LIFE IS A GARDEN TO CULTIVATE

The ABC's Towards a Better Life

PASCUALA HERRERA

FOREWORD BY
Stacey Watson, MA, LCPC, and
Christopher Watson, PsyD, ABPP

ISBN 979-8-9865567-0-3

To view personal photos and more, please visit Pascuala online at pascualaherrera.com.

Cover design: 100Covers
Interior design: Formatted Books
Edited by Allison Felus

Printed in the United States of America

CONTENTS

DEDICATION

To my granddaughter, Aria Virginia Velasquez, who, God willing, will join us in life before the end of the year. May the lessons your grandmother learned prepare you to live a beautiful and joyous life.

And to my family and friends who are always ready to support me and to give me strength.

In memory of Van Bensett, a Life Directions friend, who worked tirelessly to assist so many young adults live a better life.

FOREWORD

My husband and I were honored to meet Pascuala Hererra in 2006 at Harper College in Palatine, Illinois. I was hired as an adjunct faculty in the Office of Disabilities to counsel students in a post-secondary setting. I am a Licensed Clinical Professional Counselor with expertise in working with students with physical and mental health disabilities. I also codeveloped Project TAP at Harper College for helping students on the autism spectrum make the transition to post-secondary education. At Harper College I had a secondary role teaching classes in both the Human Services and Student Development departments. Currently, I am in private practice working with the same population, as well as an adjunct faculty at National Louis University. My husband, Dr. Christopher Watson, is a board-certified child and adolescent psychologist who has been in private practice for eighteen years. He trains parents and school systems to use the Collaborative and Proactive Solutions approach.

In 2006 when I met Pascuala, I knew instantly that she was a woman of distinction. We would spend hours talking about her past accomplishments, current achievements, and future projects. Pascuala and I would discuss her life journey and all the obstacles she had to overcome to become the woman she is today. She said she might have been discouraged at times, but she fought hard and overcame those obstacles. Pascuala would spend countless hours working with students over the years. She would always teach students with disabilities to look past their disability and focus on their strengths. I knew from the beginning that I had to introduce my husband to Pascuala.

For the next twelve years, my husband and I had the privilege of collaborating with Pascuala on common students, projects, and presentations. We were able to co-teach classes for students with disabilities on how to be their own personal advocate. We also traveled all over the country speaking at conferences about the importance of the first year of college for students with disabilities in making their transition to adulthood. During our travels, my husband and I were able to witness firsthand the challenges that individuals with disabilities had with accessibility. Pascuala would always keep a positive spirit and explained to us that this was the reason she was advocating for the rights of individuals with disabilities.

This is the third book Pascuala Herrera has authored. We loved her first book, *Not Always a Valley of Tears: A Memoir of a Life Well Lived*. This firsthand account takes the reader on a personal journey which details the successes Pascuala achieved when the odds were against her. This book also focuses on the power of faith and family. My husband and I were very touched by her honesty about her life's journey. We also loved her second book, *My Mom Rocks: Her Chair Rolls*, a children's book. It is an amazing look into the life of a child who has a parent with a disability. It is an inspiration and support for other children who have parents with disabilities and shows them that their life and experiences aren't so different from others'.

This brings us to Pascuala's present work. *Life Is a Garden to Cultivate* is for any reader wanting encouragement and motivation to live their best life. Pascuala draws upon her many years of personal and professional experience to share with her readers. She writes in a way that is thought provoking and captures the true meaning of resilience. This book uses the alphabet to allow the reader to remember life lessons related to that letter. In today's world where individuals need hope and encouragement, *Life Is a Garden to Cultivate* delivers both in a powerful way.

My husband and I were so honored to be asked to write this foreword because of our expertise in the field of mental health and disability studies. We were also asked because of the professional relationship that we have had with Pascuala Herrera since 2006. We know that every word written comes from her many years of personal and professional experience. Pascuala continues to share her passion for disability rights and encourages readers to be their best self. She encourages her readers to remember that life is not always easy but that each individual has the power to reach their goals.

Stacey Watson, MA, LCPC, and
Christopher Watson, PsyD, ABPP

PREFACE

On the first day of my summer 2021 vacation in California, when trying to transfer from my wheelchair onto the bed, I fell and, landing forcefully on my left knee, fractured my tibia and fibula bones. Up to now, I have had ten broken bones during my life.

After a rough year of COVID and the pandemic that the whole world unexpectedly experienced, my family decided to go on a much-needed vacation in July 2021. The only downside was that my oldest daughter, Ariel, would not be able to accompany us because she had a new job and was going to take care of the furry members of our family. Because my husband and I are retired, and Ariana, my youngest daughter, was on summer break from school, we decided to make it a two-week adventure, to make up for the year we did not vacation. We had so much to celebrate! Isidro and I had retired; I had received faculty emeritus status from Harper College; I successfully published *Not Always a Valley of Tears* I co founded Educators 4 Equity and Justice with two friends; Ariel was in a healthy, steady relationship with a nice young man; and Ariana had finished her third year of college.

We decided to go to Las Vegas for the first week because Isidro and I would be celebrating our twenty-sixth wedding anniversary and that is where we first met, and because Ariana had turned twenty-one in June making her legal for a casino environment. We planned to spend the second week in Anaheim, California. Ariana had always wanted to go to Hollywood and to the Disney California Adventure Park, and we all loved the beautiful weather in California.

We decided to drive, not because of the cost of flying, but because having our own vehicle provides our family more access to get around because it is modified for wheelchairs which I use because of my disability. And besides, our family has always enjoyed road trips. We knew it would be a long drive, but we were in no hurry and had planned stops along the way. In the past, we had driven multiple times to Miami and Texas which were also far in distance from Chicago.

We arrived in Vegas on June 27, 2021, and checked into our beautiful hotel that had eleven restaurants and a big spacious casino. Another attraction of the hotel was that it was a stop on the monorail that connected us to all the other hotels on the strip. We had so much fun! We visited most of the big hotels, exploring each stop of the monorail. On our anniversary, July 1, we went downtown to visit the Plaza Hotel where Isidro and I had met over twenty-six years before.

Our twenty-sixth wedding anniversary was so special! We strolled around downtown, had a delicious dinner, did some shopping, and of course, played the slots at the Golden Nugget. We felt that we were in an ideal place in our lives—happy and grateful for so much. We were happy that we had made it to Las Vegas safely, happy that we had survived a tough pandemic year, happy that we had accomplished so much as a family, and grateful that we had the means to splurge for a fun family vacation.

The next day, July 2, we left Las Vegas and drove five hours to Anaheim, California. We checked in at 4 PM and grabbed brochures from the hotel lobby to plan our activities for the week. I unpacked, and we decided to order pizza and just rest from our trip. At about 7 PM we placed the pizza order, so I got down from the bed into my wheelchair to go to the bathroom and wash my hands for dinner. Afterward, I came back to the bed, taking my time to transfer because the bed was high, which they often are in hotels. (Typically, a hotel's definition of accessibility is not always my definition.) As I stood on my right leg and was maneuvering to get onto the bed—something I had already successfully done earlier—my right leg slipped, causing me to fall forcefully onto my left knee. I screamed in pain, "I broke it; I broke it!" Both Isidro and

Ariana tried to calm me down, but I knew it was broken. The pain of a broken bone is unmistakable!

Isidro had the hotel call the paramedics, and they came at once (before the pizza). I was in excruciating pain but hoped that maybe it was just a bad sprain (which I have also experienced in the past). The paramedics lifted me up and laid me on the bed. When I told the paramedics that I didn't want to be taken to the hospital, they recommended that I ice my injury and rest it to see if the pain would be alleviated. But the icing and rest did not help; I spent the entire night in the kind of pain that sent chills up my spine if I moved my left leg in certain positions. In the hours of the dark night, all I could do was think. I recalled all the falls in my life, all my broken bones, and all the suffering I had experienced in the past. I cried as I asked, "God, why? Why again? I already have mobility issues, why give me more?"

The next morning I knew I had to go to the emergency room to find out if my leg was broken, since it was very swollen and the pain had not subsided. Isidro and I talked, and we decided that we best head home because, even with the best-case scenario, I probably would have to stay in bed. Ariana and Isidro packed the bags and we checked out and went to the nearby hospital. My leg was x-rayed, and it showed that I had fractured two bones—the tibia and the fibula of my left leg. I guess I am an overachiever even when it comes to broken bones.

The doctor, knowing that I was from out of state, stabilized my leg using a temporary boot. He then directed me to see an orthopedic doctor at home so that he/she could decide if surgery was needed and, if not, to determine what would be the best treatment plan. The hospital staff were amazing, assisting me into my van and helping me find a way to sit with my leg straight. Using our creativity and items intended for other purposes, such as a hospital transfer board and straps, I was finally settled as best as possible for the long ride home. I was given pain medicine and we started on our 2,000 mile, twenty-eight-hour journey home.

Typically, I help Isidro with driving but this time he had to do the drive entirely on his own since Ariana is not a highway driver nor comfortable driving my huge, heavy van. Isidro knew we could not stop at a hotel for the night, so he drove straight through. I didn't take my pain medication because I wanted to stay vigilant to ensure that Isidro would be wide awake and alert. It took us thirty-six hours to get home, only stopping for gas, bathroom, and food. Of course, my limitations added time to the drive. We arrived home at 4 AM on a Monday morning, which was also a holiday because of the Fourth of July. I had stayed in the same position for the entire thirty-six-hour trip.

I have no idea how we managed to get me out of the van. However, as soon as I laid my head on my bed, I was out. All the pain, stress, and worry I endured during the long drive knocked me out. I slept until noon. I called my doctor and he suggested I wait until the next day to see an orthopedic doctor. He said that going to the emergency room was unnecessary because all they would do was to diagnose the broken bones, which the hospital in California had already done.

On Tuesday, after going to the doctor my primary doctor referred me to, I was casted from my toes to my upper thigh. Fortunately, because the orthopedic doctor didn't fear that I would move a lot because of my disability, he concluded that surgery would not be necessary and recommended a cast instead. I was in a cast for eight weeks. As always, I tried to look at the silver lining of everything—and although sometimes it takes me longer than other times, I eventually do. As I reflected on my difficult ordeal, I was grateful no surgery was needed. Also, I was appreciative that I was able to continue with my already scheduled memoir presentations because they had been booked as virtual. Above all, I was thankful and felt blessed to have my family and friends ready to help me with the two difficult months of recovery.

Even after acknowledging my blessings and all the reasons to be grateful, though, I couldn't help but to feel depressed, falling into a deep valley of tears. I couldn't understand why my life changed from one day to the other. Over and over, I asked, "Why? What is the lesson for me? Is it to humble me and remind me that I should never take anything for granted?" I was not completely sure of the purpose behind this most scary and difficult incident. Sometimes, I even thought that it was not fair. However, all I could do was to ask for strength and patience as it was likely that for months I would be totally dependent on others as I waited for the healing process of my broken bones. I was sad; of course I was. But I prayerfully and patiently waited until the "why" of what happened to me could be revealed. I had faith that God had a reason! Fortunately, I arrived at the conclusion that even with my limited mobility and disability, I am blessed, and that my situation could have always been worse. It also encouraged me to think that perhaps my experience could motivate others to realize that we must all enjoy each happy moment to the fullest because things can change instantly.

Often, as I wait for these answers, I take the time to reflect on my life and happiness. My focus is to search for what really matters and change my pessimistic feelings so that I can have the best life journey possible. I always remember that when negative things happen in our lives, we have only two options. One option is to change what happened, which I knew I couldn't. The second option is to change how I responded to what was happening. That, I could do. Reflecting on my situation led me to find my solution. Life, after all, is a garden that needs constant cultivation. It is through reflection and making the required changes that we will be led to a better chance of living a happy and fulfilled life.

ACKNOWLEDGMENTS

I could list the people I am grateful for, but I wouldn't have enough space. I have always been blessed to have others in my life who help me carry my burdens. I've become who I am because of my family, friends, coworkers, students, and even the strangers I've encountered. A helping hand is always near. My only recompense is to give honor to this by never giving up and by continuing to work toward having a fulfilled life despite my challenges, obstacles, and suffering. God has given me my share of challenges, but he has rewarded me beyond measure. Although at times I have felt that my life has been too difficult, it doesn't take me long to realize that if I do my part, God is always by my side. Of course, I could not have published this book without the professional support from my copy editor, Allison Felus.

INTRODUCTION

It has taken me my entire life so far to finally understand that I have been chasing something that does not exist except when I personally and intentionally make it happen. Happiness does not just fall in our laps. Sometimes, I am sure, we all wish it would! In life, most people, if not all, strive to be happy, yet few, if any, ever reach true happiness. We all seek to reach the feeling of euphoria, but that feeling of joy, fulfillment, and pleasure doesn't come as often as we wish it would. And even when it does come, very few of us can manage to stay in the happy state for too long. I have asked myself if happiness is real, obtainable, and possible. Or, is happiness just a desired state that is an illusion that can never be obtained? The answer is that it depends on us in the way we live our lives.

As I reflect on my own life, I will share the ABCs of what usually brings me most fulfillment and purpose. I use the power that I, like all humans, have, to choose happiness over despair. I do admit that sometimes, because I am human, I do not follow these important concepts because I would much rather complain and delve into the dark side of sadness, anger, and despair. Thankfully, I choose not to stay in this negative state for too long.

I acknowledge that we are human, and we cannot entirely avoid negativity when we go through a difficult moment. By no means do I have all the answers. I am constantly cultivating my own life's garden. Just like a beautiful garden, the work is never easy or complete. I am not a counselor, a psychologist, or a psychiatrist. What I present are my opinions based on my personal experiences with my family and friends and what I have learned professionally from college students with disabilities after my thirty-year career as an educator. My goal is not for readers to think as I do, nor do I hope to change readers' perspectives. My only desire is that this book serves as a tool for readers to reflect on their own lives. Sometimes, we need reminders of the importance of being gentle with ourselves. Sometimes we need others to provide nurturing support. Sometimes, we just need to see the light. I hope this book helps readers to consider reflection as a way to shine light on the areas where they most need personal growth.

I have found that by cultivating my most important garden, my life, and by reflecting on these ABCs, I have been regularly led to personal growth and a better life. It helped me see my life clearly so that I can make changes that can get me back on the right track. Reflection allows me to stop being a victim and instead take control again. I use the ABCs just to organize my thoughts. Each letter will cover a word standing for a feeling, a value, or a concept that has lead me to live a purposeful and happy life despite the many difficult moments I have experienced in my life.

Sometimes it was difficult to choose just one word. This book will also be available in Spanish as a direct translation, therefore I had to choose words that started with the same letter and had the same meaning in both languages. Some letters provided many options whereas with some letters I had to use my creativity. I hope that all readers will connect with some or all the ideas I present, helping them to reflect on their own lives and embrace the power within all of us to make the right choices. I will use my personal experiences, some painful but some funny, along with stories of others such as family, friends, and many of my past students who have all been important in my life's journey. For confidentiality purposes, I have changed some names unless I received direct permission from the person. I also only use first names. The stories will showcase how our happiness and success are entirely in our own hands.

After each topic, I have included reflection questions. These questions can be explored either independently or within a group setting; they can serve as good discussion questions and conversation starters. Readers may come up with other discussion questions based on their own thinking and reading of each chapter. I encourage them to include the additional questions, which I know will result in thought-provoking discussions.

CHAPTER 1
ATTITUDE

IF YOU'RE ANYTHING LIKE ME, YOU HAVE PROBABLY READ MANY SLOGANS and messages about attitude. I have even collected some because they serve as good reminders for me. But I debated if I should start the book with this concept since many may see it as repetitious or even trite. However, I ultimately decided to write about attitude because I know that a negative outlook has the potential to make us miserable and a cheerful outlook has the potential to make us content. Think about it: how is it that some people who have difficult lives because of lack of resources, poor health, or other difficulties often seem happier than those who have all the resources they need, are healthy, and may otherwise have a good life? I have met many people who show happiness regardless of their life situation. I strive to be one of those people.

In my own experience, I have often noticed that just by changing my attitude, I change my state of mind and circumstances. In my preface I shared how I recently broke two bones while on vacation in California. I was miserable for a couple of weeks. My misery was not because of a ruined vacation or even because of the pain I was suffering. Rather, my misery was because for the first two weeks of my injury, I was feeling sorry for myself. My attitude was negative! Understandably, I was unhappy with my situation and felt that I was the only person suffering in the world. I couldn't comprehend why I had to endure this experience again and was angry at myself, my life, and everything that surrounded me. I did not allow any hope or positivity during those weeks of being self-absorbed. However, when I changed my attitude, I was able to see that sad things happen to people all the time. I was able to acknowledge that some people even have more difficult lives than I do. Why should I be the exception, safeguarded from suffering? Reflecting on this, I realized that I have a great life, much better than so many others—disability, broken leg, and all.

With this change of attitude, I was able to see the beauty of what was happening to me. I was able to see the blessings that surrounded me. I have a wonderful family that was willing to support me in different ways, which is not something everyone has. Some sisters cooked for me; others helped with my personal care such as washing my hair. Family members would help with getting groceries and even in doing chores around my house. And the beauty of it all is that I didn't even have to ask. They were there because of the love they feel for me. How can I not acknowledge how blessed I am?

Friends supported me also by visiting and by listening to me. They showed their concern for me with encouraging cards, texts, calls, and messages. I discovered that I was not alone once I shifted my attitude from negativity to positivity. Above all, I realized that, from my own bed, I had the tools I needed to be fulfilled. It was my choice to use them or not. Thankfully, because of my change in attitude, I used everything that was within my reach. While I was bedridden, I was able to work virtually even while casted and totally immobile. I was able to continue to do my book presentations, conduct the meetings that were necessary, and talk to others through Zoom or other similar platforms. Two broken bones did not take away my ability to use the technology available at my fingertips. Instead of focusing on what I couldn't do, I focused on what I could do. I made the decision to use the time to write and publish a children's book, *My Mom Rocks: Her Chair Rolls*, with versions in both English and Spanish. Had I not had this experience, I would not have published the children's book when I did. Could this have even been the reason why this terrible event happened to me?

Attitude is everything. It is what makes us succeed or fail. It is what makes us sad and miserable or happy and accomplished. Best of all, we are 100% in control of our emotions. Sometimes we must dig in deep, and it may take a while to change a negative attitude, but once it's changed, we have the power to see all that is good around us. By changing our attitudes, we can see our circumstances differently. Because of my change in attitude, I was able to openly see my blessings and became grateful for them.

Today, as I sit in my garden and start to write this first chapter about attitude, I can't help but smile as I remember an incident that happened last summer when I was totally dependent on others. Due to the success of my memoir, the local high school wanted to feature me on a video. I was thrilled and did not want to miss this great opportunity. However, I feared that, with my medical situation and being in a full-length cast, I wouldn't be able to participate in the recording of the video. But because of my change in attitude, I thought about solutions and not impossibilities.

Another problem that concerned me about recording the video was my gray hair. I worried about looking older than I am because of my hair. For years, I have colored my hair every month, but now I wasn't able to color it because of the cast and my lack of mobility. But my two daughters and my niece Estela encouraged me. Estela said, "Come on, Tia Cuali [Cuali is my nickname], we are smart ladies; we can figure out a way to color your hair." With a negative attitude, I would have probably rejected the offer, feeling sorry for myself. However, with my changed attitude, I accepted.

We scheduled the grand makeover day. My brother Lalo helped by manufacturing a steel plate at his job that allowed me to sit in my wheelchair with my leg sticking out. Estela, her daughter Lily, and my daughters Ariel and Ariana were ready to transform my grayish hair into beautiful auburn hair. By using a huge garbage can and a funnel they invented made from thick plastic, they figured out how to get rid of my worry by making me beautiful for the video. So, leaning back in my wheelchair, under my peach tree, the girls colored my hair outside in my yard. I told them, "I am sure no one has ever had their hair colored under a peach tree." To celebrate the happy moment, I reached up and grabbed a peach (even though it wasn't even ripe yet!) and began eating it while they rinsed my hair.

By changing my attitude, it allowed me to experience happiness even in the midst of my less-than-ideal situation. Not only that, but with my change of attitude, I found solutions for my obstacles instead of giving up. I could not change my situation, but I could change my response to it. Additionally, it allowed me to focus on my abilities, so I used the time to write and publish a book instead of focusing on all that I couldn't do. My attitude change accomplished all of this, making me feel so much better. I would not have had this power without shifting from negativity to positivity and changing my response to what was happening to me.

Shifting from a negative attitude to a positive attitude is not easy. Sometimes the situation is so difficult that we may get stuck in the darkness for longer than we wish. Looking back at my life, I remember two situations that took me longer to change how I was feeling. One situation was when I lost a son due to a premature birth after I had already had two failed pregnancies. Those were dark moments, and the grief took me prisoner. I felt as if I would never be happy again. The pain was raw. I remember feeling miserable, and I even hated seeing happy people. I would ask myself, "How can they be happy when I am so stricken with pain?" However, time passed and amazingly, even this type of pain healed. And now, looking back, I am even grateful for those dark moments. Because of those painful losses, my husband and I were open to different ways of becoming parents and decided to adopt a child. Now I cannot see my life without Ariel, my beautiful adopted daughter. So sometimes, we must remember that if we are patient, the dark times of our lives may lead us to unexpected happiness.

Another time when I struggled to change my attitude was after the most significant woman in my life, my mother, passed away. She was my everything. I depended on her emotionally and physically. She would be the first person I'd seek for support and encouragement. I knew that we had a special bond ever since I was diagnosed with polio as an infant. She made it her life's mission to support me and to help me make my dreams come true. I was equally connected with her, and sometimes I would move forward just because I wanted her to be happy.

After her death, I wondered how I would ever heal from such a tremendous loss. Again, time took care of it. We just celebrated the fourth anniversary of her departure, and though the pain is still there, I am now able to see it with resignation and acceptance. In fact, her loss led me to delve into writing and publishing. I wrote a memoir as a tribute to her and all that she did for me so that I could get to where I am in life today. So again, my attitude was changed by time. What I used to see as dark and negative, I can now see as bright and peaceful. I am grateful that I had her as my mom. Knowing that she is no longer suffering and that she is in a better place brings me peace.

The negative attitudes of others have often affected my life as a Mexican immigrant woman with a disability. My every day is met by these negative attitudes that sometimes blatantly depict the biases toward those like me who are different. Some people cannot understand how my life can be plentiful even without my ability to walk. They express those biases in very hurtful ways, sometimes seeing me as less than or, even worse, making me feel invisible. These reactions hurt; however, I use the power over my own attitude and decide not to allow these incidents define or otherwise determine how I should see myself. The ability to do this has taken time and practice. As a younger child, adolescent, and young adult, it was difficult for me to block people's negative attitudes toward me, which often left scars on my self-confidence. As an older adult, I am now more capable of recognizing that others' attitudes toward me is a problem *they* have, and I can again decide not to let them hurt me. Often, instead, I choose to take it as an opportunity for a teachable moment in which I can point out how their behavior is discriminatory and/or hurtful.

Attitudes of others can have a big impact on people, even on those we love. As an educator, I often saw how a parent's attitude toward their child unintentionally affected that student's success. Some parents totally denied the difficulties a student experienced because of their disability. The parents instead expected their children to pursue the careers that the parents wanted for them, without recognizing that these aspirations might be unrealistic or that the areas of study were not what the student wanted. Their attitude was that the student could have a lucrative career regardless of their child's disability and how they were impacted by it. Their attitude was one of entitlement.

As a person with a disability, I of course understood that a disability should not determine a person's future. However, I do believe that, regardless of the label of disability, not every student, with *or* without disabilities, can have whatever career they want. Every person has abilities and difficulties. Some are good with math while others are good with reading and writing. Some are good with sciences, yet others are good with hands-on skills. For instance, sometimes parents wanted their student, who was placed in the lowest level of math, to become an engineer. It was challenging to try to explain why this was an unrealistic goal for the student and even more difficult to change the parents' attitudes.

Other parents had a contrary viewpoint, which was equally hard on the student. Parents believed that college was not for their students, whether because of their poor academic history or previous difficulties because of their disability. I noticed this way of thinking in many of the Latino families I served. They would often come to me because I spoke Spanish and would make comments like "My son is horrible in school. He should just go to work at my husband's factory" or "School is not for her. She can't learn." Similarly, I would strive to change their negative attitudes, making them believe that an education was fundamental to their student's success in life. Most would listen to my opinion and were happy that a Latina was encouraging them because they, like most parents, wanted what was best for their child. My hope was that I could change one attitude at a time.

By no means do I think that changing attitudes can happen naturally and quickly. I am sure each person must go through his, her, or their own process, just like I did. It is hard work. What I know for certain, however, is that staying in a depressed and negative state does not resolve the issues we are experiencing. Quite the contrary—it makes the situation worse. I have learned that the longer I have a negative attitude, the longer I take to heal and move forward. This, of course, depends on our willingness to allow light in. For me, this happens with the support of family and friends and with my faith and prayers.

As a college professor at a community college for thirty years, I have also had the opportunity to witness how positive attitudes often determined a student's success. I was always amazed by how students with severe learning difficulties, but with positive attitudes and motivation, would sometimes be more successful than those with higher cognitive abilities but poor attitudes. My goal was to always support students by guiding them to change how they viewed their disabilities, teaching them that a disability didn't have to be what determined their success. Sometimes I was successful in my guidance, and I was rewarded by seeing how these students flourished, then later became examples of success stories.

Tammy is just one of those many students I had the privilege of working with. She started at Harper College after a difficult high school experience. When she started her first semester, she brought with her the negative experiences of being bullied and made to feel not worthy of success. As I worked with her, I kept reminding her that the college offered her a clean slate where she could be the writer of her own journey and that it could be a story of success. With this new hope, she worked hard and was patient as she navigated her education. She was successful in completing a degree, moving forward to a higher degree at a university. Now she is a successful teacher, helping students like herself, who were made to believe that they could not succeed.

Another student, Steve, had served time in prison, and when he was released, he came to Harper. He, too, brought his history of difficulties with school along with his experience of serving time in a prison. He shared that he had always hated school due to his severe reading disabilities. He knew he had to change his life after his experience with prison, so he sought support from my department. As I worked with Steve, it was evident that he needed to learn that we all have different talents and abilities. I explained that he could reach success even with his difficulties with reading. He was so excited to know that there were career fields that would focus on skills he could excel in and that there were tools and technologies to compensate for skills in which he struggled. Steve completed a certificate in welding and now works as a welder making a sufficient income to support his wife and child. The change of attitude from "I can't do anything" to "I can do some things" was all it took for him to succeed.

However, there were students who were unable or even unwilling to change their attitudes, falling victim to what they thought others believed of them. This often resulted in not being successful, ending up on academic probation, and/or later quitting college. Unfortunately, though they likely possessed what was necessary for success, they were unable to believe in themselves no matter what I did. A change in how they viewed themselves could have made all the difference between success and failure. No matter how much I wanted every student to succeed, attitudes can only be controlled by each person individually. I could not change their attitudes for them!

Our own attitudes and the attitudes of others can change our views of life. Being aware of our negativity, though, can greatly spotlight the changes we need to make so that we can see things differently. The situation does not change, because most of the time, these situations are out of our control. But we do control our feelings, our outlook, and how we respond to what is happening in our lives. This change may be the key to noticing the small joyful moments that we would not notice if we did not change our attitude. The power is in all of us. We can choose darkness over light. We can choose sadness over joy. It is all up to us and no one else.

REFLECTION QUESTIONS

1. What are examples where your attitude affected you negatively?
2. What are examples where your attitude affected you positively?
3. How do other people's attitudes affect you either positively or negatively?
4. What will you do to change your negative attitude and improve your outlook?

CHAPTER 2
BEAUTY

WE HAVE ALL HEARD THE SAYING "BEAUTY IS IN THE EYE OF THE BE-holder." Our opinions about what is beautiful and what is not vary. The harm comes when we fall for and believe in society's view of what is beautiful. We know society's view of beauty includes having the perfect body, having the perfect complexion, and having a spectacular style and look. But how many of us really fit this image? I do not. As a person with a disability, I've often felt that people did not see me as beautiful, no matter who I was inside, how I dressed, or all that I had accomplished. When I google images for the word *beautiful*, I will never see someone even vaguely resembling me.

Growing up in a Mexican family, I would often sit down to watch novelas (Spanish soap operas) with my mom. I was always observant of how the actresses playing the various parts would have the perfect hair, the perfect body, and would wear stylish and expensive clothes, often even when just waking up in the morning. All of them were drop-dead gorgeous. The men on the soaps were muscular, none of them with beer bellies or unkempt hair. Every single actor was tall, slim, and handsome. No matter the station or novela, people were depicted following society's definition of beauty.

As a young woman, I often wondered why they didn't show women who didn't have a perfect body or why, on the rare occasion they did show someone with a disability, the character was always depicted as unhappy because of their physical condition. They either wanted to die or prayed for a miracle that would give them the ability to walk. Was it because novelas were meant to entertain and were just make-believe? Or was it because disability was viewed as something ugly that must be gotten rid of in order to be happy? Regardless, I know my self-image was affected negatively because I never saw anyone on television who resembled me or who was shown being happy despite having a disability. It was a constant battle within myself because every message I received was that having a disability was bad or ugly.

Wouldn't it be nice if people judged others by more important qualities than physical beauty? I question how this would affect our young people who strive to reach the coveted beauty standards that our society depicts yet are so unrealistic. As humans, we always try to fit in, but why do we believe that the only way to fit in is to achieve some standard of beauty imposed on us? We fall into the trap of getting on the next fad diet, buying designer clothes we cannot afford, contemplating cosmetic surgery, and eventually becoming depressed because we are still so far from fitting that beauty ideal.

I recall how much I suffered wanting to be beautiful in the ways that I perceived others saw beauty. I spent countless hours feeling sorry for myself and blaming my disability for my lack of beauty. I would be embarrassed by the leg braces and shoes I wore because of my polio, and the braces and crutches also limited the type of clothing I could wear. Even when I was in a wheelchair and no longer used my leg braces, I had limitations that impeded my ability to fit into most of the current styles. Then, because of my disability, I couldn't exercise, so it was difficult for me to lose weight. Bottom line, my body was less than "normal." I put normal in quotation marks because, again, society has built this false structure of what is considered normal and what is considered beautiful. Very few of us can ever reach normality.

When I was in my twenties, I really struggled with wanting normalcy. I remember going out with my friends to parties or concerts and noticing how, when my girlfriends and I went to the bathroom (yes, often in a group), they would also check their makeup, fix their hair, and do a lipstick touch-up. I wouldn't do any of those things. First, I couldn't because the vanities were often inaccessible, and I couldn't see my reflection in the mirrors. Second, even if I could see my reflection in a mirror, I was too self-conscious and thought I would be judged. I imagined that everybody else would be shocked that I would even think of checking the mirror to try to make myself more attractive. These bathroom experiences were not comfortable at all, and often I got out feeling sorrier for myself than usual.

Now that I am much older and, yes, wiser, I understand that I was wrong to think I would ever be beautiful the way society depicts beauty. When my siblings started to get married, I thought that marrying was not in my future because I wasn't beautiful enough. I am blessed that I was proven wrong in my belief that I lacked beauty enough to be marrying material. My husband Isidro was able to see my inner and outer beauty. To him, there is no other woman as beautiful as me. This of course is because of love. Love transforms everything.

I admit that sometimes I still fall in the trap of wanting to be what I am not. My daughter Ariel recently got married. As I helped her plan the wedding, my greatest worry was that I would never fit the image of the "mother of the bride." How could I when I was in a wheelchair and looked the way I did? I searched for a dress that would work for me in countless bridal magazines, but I wish I hadn't looked at them at all. Instead of helping me, they depressed me even more. All the women depicted in the magazines were wearing glamorous dresses and high heels, with perfect makeup and hair. Unfortunately, I was so stressed, the worry started to consume my every thought, and I missed out on so many happy moments of preparing for my daughter's wedding.

As I often do, though, I decided to change my thinking since I could not change the fact that I would never look like the models in the magazines. I decided to find a solution instead of feeling sorry for myself. So, I reflected on what I needed and figured out a way to look beautiful in my own way. I bought material to design a skirt, and with help from my nephew's wife, we created a garment that worked perfectly. Traditional skirts would not work for me because I would be unable to use the bathroom without getting the skirt wet when transferring to the toilet. So, as I now joke, I invented a curtain for my lap! Basically, it is a skirt with a slit from top to bottom on the back. This allowed me to sit on my wheelchair and just drape the material around my legs, making it look like a "real" skirt.

I may not have fit the magazines' image of what the mother of the bride should look like, but I certainly fit in as the mother of the bride of my beautiful daughter Ariel. This change happened because I allowed myself to change my own feelings about beauty. I was the only one that was hurting myself by trying to use garments that were designed for people who are not in wheelchairs. Why should I try to fit into a world that is not for me? Why not create what is practical yet beautiful for me? This experience really helped me to reflect on how much we all strive to be like everyone else. Rarely do we allow ourselves to shine in our own beauty.

Beauty indeed is in the eye of the beholder. However, as humans, we are so critical of ourselves because we do not recognize that being different doesn't make us ugly. Being different, with different body structures, different types of hair, different skin color, different facial characteristics, can be beautiful. I recognized that the harm I did to myself was because of wanting to be the same as other women instead of celebrating myself exactly the way I am.

In my wisdom, I now see beauty differently. I have noticed how seemingly attractive individuals can be ugly on the inside and in their worldviews. Vica versa, some of the less physically attractive individuals can be the most beautiful people. Personality, behavior, intelligence, and kindness are what really make a person beautiful. The people who support and love us are the most beautiful people in our opinion. In fact, I believe that everything God created is beautiful, but we destroy that beauty with our choices and the way we live our lives. I wish I'd had this wisdom earlier in life. However, I believe that it takes time for us to comprehend how every single person in the world is a beautiful creation of God. We are here in this world to live that beauty. We will destroy our beauty by not appreciating our individuality and by always trying to be like everyone else. We must stop being our worst critics and stop comparing ourselves to others.

At the college, I worked with thousands of students. I also taught a Humanistic Psychology course that I often described as a self-esteem course. In this course, I taught on different aspects of the human experience, including topics such as body image, life stages, and motivation. Internally, I often felt like a hypocrite because I was teaching self-esteem when I, myself, had such a low self-esteem in the way I viewed myself. Interestingly, I was able to see the beauty of each one of my students, yet I couldn't see my own. Fortunately, the more I taught the course and witnessed the change in students, the more I learned how to accept myself. I believe all good educators sometimes learn more from a class than the students they're teaching. This was certainly true for me.

Being kind to ourselves is a difficult endeavor. We have been conditioned to judge ourselves harshly. As I was raising my daughters, I wanted to protect them from this reality. I wanted both of my daughters to value themselves as human beings. I knew that each of them was beautiful in their own way, but I wanted to teach them that what matters most is how they viewed themselves. I feared that being raised by two parents with disabilities would add an additional barrier to their ability to see themselves as beautiful. Our family was constantly stared at, pitied, and otherwise made to feel different. "Different" typically translates to being "ugly." I never wanted them to feel that our family was less than beautiful, even though we *were* different and not the typical family.

Now that my daughters are adults, I think my husband and I were successful in our goal. Both of my daughters, though different as night and day, know what matters most in life. They know what makes people beautiful. And they are beautiful because they are open to differences, not fast to make judgments, and respectful of all people. In their twenties, they have demonstrated that they are well grounded individuals who appreciate the beauty in themselves and others. I am very proud of them. They were raised by parents who could have caused them to feel "less than," but rather, their experience helped them appreciate what really matters in life—love, family, and kindness.

I struggled more with self-acceptance than my daughters ever did. I know that this is due to my disability and being raised by the humblest parents. My mother never thought she was beautiful. In fact, she resisted ever looking at a camera. When we took pictures of her, she would often look down, as if she was not worthy of being in the picture. As for my dad, at times he felt that, without an education, he wasn't enough. Both of my parents were the most beautiful people in the world to me and to many others. Their love for their family, their total dedication to us, and the values they instilled in us, made each of them more than precious. They proved that the beauty of the soul and spirit are more significant than any physical attributes.

I won't doubt that, on occasion, I will continue to feel less than and sometimes even ugly. However, I know that these feelings will not last long. I now know better. I know that happiness begins with accepting ourselves in the beautiful image God created. I realize that I was not born with the societal view of beauty, but that God gifted me with other beautiful qualities. I am a diligent worker, view life with a grateful heart, and am always looking for ways to live life to the fullest. I also know that I need to value my own beauty before I can appreciate the beauty of others.

REFLECTION QUESTIONS

1. What does beauty mean to you?
2. What are your best attributes?
3. Do you see yourself as beautiful, and why or why not?
4. What are instances where you didn't/don't feel beautiful?
5. How can you help yourself and others to feel beautiful?

CHAPTER 3

COURAGE

Fear, when we give it power, is the greatest cause of our suffering and unhappiness. However, having the courage to face our fears can be the source of our greatest liberation. I have lived all my life with fear. But I have been successful because I have never allowed the fear to take over my life. I have always moved forward despite fear, often resulting in success.

However, living with a disability has given me more reasons to fear. In every stage of my life, I have feared things that could have stifled my ability to move forward. As a child, I feared being different, and I lacked an understanding of why I could not go to school with my siblings but instead was forced to go to a special school. As an adolescent, trying to walk on leg braces and crutches, I feared falling, especially because my falls often resulted in broken bones. In addition, I always feared not fitting in because I saw myself as different. As an adult, I feared not being good enough to marry. Because of my disability, I feared not finding a job in my career, even with an education. I feared not being able to have children and become a mother. The list goes on, and the fears continue still today. Now I fear aging and how it will affect my mobility even more. Still, even with these fears, I have had the courage to exercise my power to go beyond those feelings and continue moving forward.

Fear is the most debilitating type of emotion. I believe that fear of failing and fear of the unknown are possibly the two greatest types of fears, but also the most common. In our minds, we make up predictions of all that could go wrong, often neglecting to predict all that could go right. I am fortunate to have discovered that, typically, even in the worst-case scenarios, what could go wrong was not as horrifying as what my mind made it out to be. So, if we just have the courage to act, even with fear, we will find that, most of the time, we are only catastrophizing the situation we are in.

Chicago's extremely harsh winters are especially challenging for individuals who need crutches, wheelchairs, or other mobility equipment. Winters can be so dangerous for individuals with mobility impairments, whose gait is compromised. I learned to drive, but fear often gripped me when I had to drive during conditions that could have easily caused me to get stuck in the snow. Another real concern for me was being involved in a car accident where I could be injured and/or be unable to get out for assistance. I am certain that my parents also experienced these same fears when they saw me leave in my vehicle during treacherous weather. However, like me, they didn't allow their fears to interfere with my doing what I had to do. I clearly remember my mom, even at an older age, helping me to my vehicle, giving me a blessing, and watching me leave. I am so fortunate that my parents modeled courage by not allowing their fears to stop me.

My parents were very courageous in more ways than one. This is true for many families who immigrate to a new place for a better life. My parents immigrated to the United States with the hopes of a better life for their family. Their courage is something I will always appreciate. I am certain that my life would not be what it is had they not made such a difficult decision. It is because of their courage that I accomplished all my goals and have been successful in this country. It is because of their example that I continue to have courage in each stage of my life.

But some of my fears were real. One day after torrential rains, the suburb where I live, which is close to the Des Plaines River, got flooded. I had several student appointments, so I did not want to miss work. I left my house to go to campus, though I was very afraid. I imagined, and hoped, that I would have the option to take a different route and avoid any streets that were inundated. But I was wrong. I didn't have any other choice but to pass through a flooded bridge near my home. Mannheim Road, the main street that leads to the highway, was bad. It looked more like a river than a street. The water came up to the tops of the tires of my van; if I had stuck my hand out the window, I would have been able to touch the water. As I feared, I got stuck and my van was practically floating. I was unable to steer the van because it just wouldn't move. As I tried to solve the problem, I knew getting out was out of the question; I wouldn't have been able to deploy my ramp and roll out in my power wheelchair since the van was surrounded by water. My wheelchair would stop functioning, or worse yet, it would float away just like my van was floating. Trying to go to work hadn't been a smart decision. When I concluded that I couldn't even try to get out, I had to decide who to call for help. The only logical choice was to call 911.

I thought to myself, "I bet the three strong, handsome firemen can manage to carry me out without my wheelchair if they tried." My daydream was interrupted when a couple of firemen came to my window. Rescuing me was not easy. The emergency personnel couldn't take me out because of my power wheelchair; it is not only heavy, but also, getting any water on it would have been dangerous, due to its electricity. So they told me to stay put and that they were going to pull me out with a rope attached to their firetruck. I was so scared, and especially embarrassed. But in my stubbornness, I thought that courage was enough. I was pulled out safely, but I learned my lesson. After this experience, I realized that sometimes it is better to play it safe. After all, even with my bravery, I still didn't get to see my students.

Taking control of fear is not easy. Anxiety does not go away even when moving forward despite our fears. However, the greatest hindrance to success is allowing fear to take control over us. For example, if I had allowed fear to take over, I would have never learned how to drive with hand controls. I would have never received an education where I was often the only one with a visible disability. Certainly, I would have never had a successful career like the one I had for thirty years. Most importantly,

I would have never had the beautiful family I now love. Even today I am constantly battling fear. If I had allowed fear to win, I would have never written and published my books. I am not fearless, though; I just have the courage to go beyond my fears, which has typically led me to success.

As our country goes through some of the most difficult times of our lives, it is now more important than ever to be courageous. With the COVID-19 pandemic, the Ukraine War, the multitude of mass shootings, and the uncertain financial situation of our country, there are, understandably, many more reasons to be fearful. But if we succumb to the fear, our lives will be more miserable. Courage does not mean that fear ceases to exist. Courage is the power we have against it.

Courage can be demonstrated in different ways. People do not have to serve in the military, although those who do show tremendous courage. I, of course, appreciate their sacrifices in making our country better by fighting so that we can freely reap the benefits and take advantage of the opportunities that the United States offers. Courage is also seen in individuals who are having all kinds of different types of battles. Perhaps people are battling illnesses or addictions. Others may be battling obstacles in living a full life despite a disability. Some may be battling barriers to make their dreams possible. Bottom line, people are always battling with something. But when we are courageous, our potential is limitless, as long as we don't limit ourselves only to safe ground. Risks are necessary!

Sometimes, fear is the greatest disability a person can have. I have often been seen as courageous because I push forward and don't let my limitations dictate what I can accomplish. I, of course, believe that this is what everyone should do. We need to get out of our comfort zones and learn to deal with the negative emotions that come with uncertainty. Again, I am probably one of the most fearful persons, but I learned to deal with the lack of comfort, the anxiety, and the thoughts about failure, and simply push those feelings down. I have concluded that my physical disability is not as disabling as the fears that stunt so many others from living their lives to the fullest. I know many people who are paralyzed, not physically, but from action because of their fears.

I remember many experiences where I wanted to give up and become a prisoner of fear. That would have been the easy route. However, I was full of dreams and, above all, I was full of faith. I always told myself, "Just work hard and leave the rest to God." This worked for me as an encouragement and motivator. No matter the challenge in front of me, I forged ahead, and I usually came out on the other end having accomplished more than I had ever thought possible. Everyone has this potential; I am not superhuman.

Probably the most difficult experience where I almost lost the battle to fear was in my attempts in becoming a mother. I knew that having polio, being in a wheelchair, and having a curvature of my spine could be great impediments to becoming a mother. But I put all those concerns aside and decided to pursue pregnancy. And, then I had two miscarriages and a premature birth of a son who only lived for two hours. This was almost too much for me to bear. Perhaps out of stubbornness, but more likely because of my deep desire to become a mother, I instead decided to pursue adoption. I ended up adopting a beautiful daughter, then getting pregnant for the fourth time, resulting in the birth of a healthy, full-term baby girl. Yes, sometimes we will fail in obtaining what we want in the way that we want it. But ultimately, even when we experience failure, there is likely a beautiful alternative solution. Courage to keep trying regardless of the fear is the answer. Sometimes our worst moments are the direct path to the best parts of our life.

My life has been full of finding alternatives. From simple tasks like bathing to more difficult chores like cooking and keeping my home clean, I have had to figure out different ways to get things done. As my disability progresses and my physical ability deteriorates, I must be creative and open to alternatives. I know this takes courage. I have regularly found life difficult, and the easy solution would have been to give up. But I never have, and I never will. I also do not always move forward alone; I utilize technology, creative self-made tools, or the help of others. Interestingly, I believe I demonstrate the greatest courage when I ask for help.

My mother was an avid gardener. She had the most beautiful garden of most neighborhoods. I always thought that gardening was not possible for me because of being in a wheelchair, so I never even appreciated the garden that my mom kept in her yard and mine. However, after her passing away, it was sad to see my yard and I missed the beauty of the flowers which I had taken for granted for many years. But my mom was gone, so I had to stop telling myself that gardening was not possible for me and instead seek out alternatives. With the help of my brother, Lalo, and a friend, I found a solution. They assisted me in transforming my garden into raised beds where I can independently plant whatever I want. I had to put aside my fear of not being able to have my own garden, and I am so glad I did because now I have the most peaceful and beautiful garden where I can reflect on my life. As a bonus, it has also allowed me to be close to my mother in a way I never thought possible.

People should ask themselves the following questions: What do I fear? Are these fears stopping me from accomplishing my goals? What can I do to take control of my fears? How can I show courage to go beyond these fears? Then simply act, and take the first step. The solution is always to just work hard. Trust me. What seemed impossible will someday be possible. It is easy to get discouraged when things do not happen when or how we want it. However, in the long run, we will accomplish more than we ever expected of ourselves. Courage is an important factor in finding happiness. When we are held back by fear, misery is assured.

Accept that fear is a human emotion. But sometimes being held back by fear is important. As a woman, I have learned to never roll alone in the dark, especially in desolate areas. Of course, we need to listen to our inner gut when it tells us there is imminent danger. Fear in this case is warranted, and we should pay attention to any internal instinct. It would be wrong to want to be courageous and risk being hurt. (I wish I had known this before attempting to go through that flooded bridge!) When I used crutches for mobility, I often opted for using a wheelchair instead during icy conditions. The fear of falling was real. It would have been ignorant of me to not pay attention to the danger of walking on crutches on icy and snowy pavements. Being courageous doesn't mean totally ignoring danger. In my case, I was not catastrophizing the possible danger. However, sometimes what we tell ourselves is not true, and we are inventing dangers when there aren't any. I am getting better at knowing the difference between real danger and danger that I only want to believe. I reflect on the differences so that I can make smarter choices and to determine if fear is stopping me from achieving my goals.

Courage is taking the risk even when the outcome is unknown. Of course, some people experience phobias which are clinically diagnosed as psychological disabilities. People diagnosed with a phobia disorder need professional treatment to be able to get through their sometimes irrational fears. But, barring a psychological condition, most of what we are afraid of stems from telling ourselves everything that could go wrong. We believe the dangers are one hundred percent real. We must differentiate when the fear is real or if it's just in our minds.

Sometimes the fears seem unreasonable but later proved to be so real. In a course I taught, I had an assignment where students had to think about their lifeline. They were to include the ups and downs of their lives. The expectation was that they would each share their lifeline in front of the class with a presentation of no longer than five minutes. Diane, one of my students, came to speak to me after class and shared that she had a great fear of public speaking. I empathized but wanted her to try to go beyond her comfort zone, reminding her that it was a safe space. She hesitantly agreed to prepare her timeline and present it at the following class.

In the following class, I checked in with Diane to see if she was still planning to present to the class. She was visibly nervous, but I reassured her and suggested she just look at me. When she went to the front of the classroom, she was shaking. She started speaking, and about a minute later, she retched, and vomited on the floor in front of her. Everyone, including me, was momentarily unable to move because of the shock. I then quickly reacted and suggested she go to the bathroom to clean up. When she left, I wasn't sure what to do since the class was on a Saturday and custodians weren't readily available. What's worse, other students with sensitive stomachs who were grossed out began gagging, running to the bathroom to throw up as well. I had no choice but to cancel the remainder of the class, since I was getting close to doing the same thing. This was a tremendous lesson for me. I learned that sometimes we need to guide students to overcome their fears, but we also should not forget to strive to keep everyone safe and not push too much.

Many of the fears I have can rationally be explained. However, repeatedly, I have proven that, with the courage to persevere and with hard work, I almost always succeed. For example, the fear I had of not being able to afford college was real. I was part of a family of eleven and my parents did not have a formal education. My mom took care of us while my dad worked in a factory, making them unable to help me with the cost of going to college. However, I didn't let that fear stop me. Instead, I looked for practical solutions, one of which was to work hard to earn scholarships. I was the only one in my family to go to college, and this happened because I moved beyond the many messages that made me doubt my ability to go to college.

Fear does serve a purpose, but we need to recognize that it is also the cause for getting us stuck and unable to move forward. Fear can be the cause of living a miserable life if we let it be in control. Sometimes our minds send false warning signs that we must ignore. Because of these fears, we often make excuses, but with reflection we will find that it's just the fear taking control of us. We must think critically about the messages we hear within ourselves. It will take courage to move despite our fears, but courage is within us all! We are stronger than we believe. And when we take control over our fears, there is great satisfaction. Courage is the antidote to fear, and it could make a world of difference in living a better life.

REFLECTION QUESTIONS

1. What are some examples of times you've shown courage?
2. What are examples of fears you have for which you need courage?
3. What steps can you take to overcome fear with courage?
4. How do you tell the difference between fear of failure and a rational fear?

CHAPTER 4

DISABILITY

I CONTEMPLATED NOT USING "DISABILITY" FOR THIS CHAPTER AND FIND-
ing another concept that begins with D. However, I opted to use it because
I want to shed light on this important concept that will impact every single
person at one time or another in life. Sure, disability has been in the forefront of my life. Being diagnosed with polio changed my life and the lives
of my entire family. However, I know that any reader of this book will also
relate to disability from personal experience, from interacting with a family
member or friend, or from caring for an aging parent.

Disability is the only minority group that people can join at any time.
It does not discriminate against gender, religious beliefs, race, social class,
or any other thinkable category. Either by birth defect, accident, disease,
or aging, anyone can join this group at any time. Even with this reality,
disability continues to be the most misunderstood, feared, and discriminated type of diversity. Regardless of the type of disability, people within
this group are often made to feel as if they do not matter in society.

For me, disability has impacted me in almost every experience, and
these experiences have made me the person I am today. Although I belong
to other marginalized groups, by no means did these identities impact my
life as much as having a disability. Being a Mexican immigrant woman

from a low-income status family didn't affect me as much as my disability. Jokingly, I have said that I didn't know I was a Latina and never thought about ways my gender was negatively viewed until I started college. And though others labeled our family as low income, we felt rich compared to what we had in Mexico. As far as I am concerned, we had moved from rags to riches.

Disability, and how others view it, has been in the forefront of all my experiences. For this reason, I never noticed how being a person of color or a woman might have also influenced the way others treated me. The world we live in was made for able-bodied individuals. It took a law, the Americans with Disabilities Act (ADA) of 1990, to begin recognizing people with disabilities as members of society who have rights just like everyone else. It was the first time that the United States took some responsibility in mandating equal treatment and access for people with disabilities. This was the first legislation prohibiting discrimination based on a disability. Even with the law, individuals like myself with disabilities often continue to be excluded from participating as equal members of society. The latest census indicates that around nineteen percent of the United States population has a form of a disability, yet inclusion continues to be a significant barrier for this targeted group.

My first twenty-five years of life were prior to the ADA being signed as law, but for more than half of my life, I have benefited from what the law mandates. So I can easily compare how my life changed because of the law. In my experience, when I was growing up, having a disability meant being segregated. And to me, separate is never equal. Because of segregation, my education was always in special schools. The constant message I received was that I needed to be fixed or at the very least separated from the "normal" kids. It's as if I was to blame for having lack of access, that it was my fault for not being like everyone else.

After the ADA became law, people with disabilities began to be integrated into schools, the public, and any entity that received federal funding. By this time, I had already completed most of my education, though I recognize that life for me as a person with a disability greatly improved with the changes the ADA mandates. Slowly I began to see the shift from blaming me for my inability to have access to making accessibility a societal responsibility. Still, I can honestly say that I continue to experience many challenges and barriers because of my disability. No doubt, we have come a long way, but we still have a long way to go. I agree that the ADA was a good start in improving the lives of Americans with disabilities because it requires a certain degree of access. However, no law can ever change other people's views of disability. People's attitudes continue to be a great barrier for the inclusion of individuals like myself who must live in and navigate a world made for those without disabilities.

It took me over fifty years of my life to finally accept that I am not faulty, less than, or in need of being fixed. This is what I used to think, based on how others around me interacted with me. Coming from Mexico and immediately getting the label of "disabled" marked my life. I couldn't understand why I was being treated differently than others. As a child, I resisted the label and often wished that I wouldn't belong to the disabled group. However, now I realize that I was never the one with the problem. I am perfectly happy not being able to walk. People may even doubt my honesty when I say this, but from the bottom of my heart I mean it.

Having a disability has been a gift for me. It has afforded me a much better understanding of the human experience, no matter how diverse it is. I am more accepting of others and believe that all of us are in this world for a reason. My disability led me to experiences which I would have never had, had I not contracted polio. I attribute my success to my disability. To live a full life, I have learned that I am gifted with other qualities that are more important than being able to walk. Because of my disability, I obtained an education. None of my siblings went to college, because they got married or entered the workforce. Because of my disability, I became an advocate and activist for the rights of those who are marginalized. As a disabled individual, I was led to the perfect career of helping students with disabilities. My disability led me to find the perfect partner for me. I met and married the love of my life, who also happens to have a disability. Having polio and being a wheelchair user caused me to have difficulties in becoming a mother, making me more open to the idea of becoming an adoptive parent. And, because of my disability, I have a perfect platform for speaking, writing, and advocating for positive change. This platform allows me to continue making my mark and making a difference in people's lives.

For all these reasons, I accept myself fully, disability and all. Sure, my life is more difficult. But it is difficult because of others' response to me and because I must live in an inaccessible environment. When I wake up each morning, I never complain about having to live another day in a wheelchair. Sometimes, I even forget about my disability. I go about my day fully forgetting my disability, and it is not until I encounter a barrier that I am reminded of it. Because my home and vehicle are accessible, and I have all the mobility aids I need to be independent, I live quite a full and active life.

I was meant to have a disability. It was my destiny. God chose me to be disabled, but he also gifted me with an outgoing personality, a hard work ethic, and a tremendous energy and passion for encouraging those around me to see the world differently. I know that some able-bodied individuals do not use their talents and choose to complain about their lives instead. Life is difficult for everyone, but it is up to us to use what we have to make a difference. All of us were dealt a poker hand of cards. At the end, those who played their cards well are winners. The people who strategically and passionately respond to whatever they were handed are ultimately the greatest winners. I know some of us must work harder and must endure much more, but in the end, we are stronger and become better human beings.

Disability is often seen by many as something scary. This is in part because of the way mass media depicts people with disabilities, which influences mainstream views and likely increases fear. How many times have we seen movies where injured and disabled characters want to die rather than to live a life with their disability? This promulgates the notion that death is preferable over living with a disability. I can tell everyone now: I do not want to die. I want to live a long and happy life. Life is worth living for all of us!

I am not going to deny that there have been times when I wished my life could be easier. This feeling often comes out of frustration. Sometimes my body cannot keep up with my mind's energy, and this results in frustration. I want to do so many things, but I most often recognize that my limitations prohibit me from doing them. I also sometimes lack patience, and I want to get things done now! Sit me in front of a computer where my brain is in charge, and there is no stopping me. However, when a task requires my physical ability, that is where I am reminded of my disability, making me feel frustrated because I either cannot get the task done or I must depend on someone else for assistance.

I call it the Herrera curse, or maybe the Herrera blessing. My mother modeled a work ethic that is sometimes difficult to follow, but all my siblings and I try to mirror that ethic by also being hard workers. She used all her gifts and was tireless in all she did. She juggled so many responsibilities because of my large family. She would wake up at the crack of dawn and be the last one to go to bed. She cleaned, cooked, cared for us, and this remained true until close to her death. Her life mission was to serve whoever entered her cozy home.

My mother passed away in April 2018, and that previous summer, when she was 84, she was still carrying heavy flowerpots, digging, and caring for her plants and all of us. Any time we went to visit her, the first thing she did was to offer us food. She was still regularly making homemade tortillas because she always wanted them available to offer her children, grandchildren, great-grandchildren, as well as any other visitor. If she wanted something done, she did it. It didn't matter her strength or her age, she would still move furniture when she wanted to reorganize. So, like her, I don't let my limitations stop me.

My disability travels with me everywhere I go. I am certain that is what people see first when they encounter me. I often felt that this was less than beneficial and have often said that I wish people would see *me* first, and not my disability. However, after many years of working with students with invisible disabilities such as learning disabilities, attention deficit disorder, and psychological disabilities, I discovered that having a visible disability is preferable to me most of the time. First, I do not have to explain myself. People will know right away that I may not be able to participate in an inaccessible environment. Second, once I discovered that my disability molded me to be the person I am today, I accept that I am fine with people seeing me as a disabled woman.

Individuals with invisible disabilities are likely most often misunderstood. They must navigate their lives with others questioning why they struggle, blaming them for lack of effort or dedication. A person with an invisible disability also needs to make the decision of whether to disclose or not. Typically, this decision is based on the person's experience, whether negative or positive. Whereas, in some instances, hiding a disability can be the best decision, such as in a job interview, often keeping it in secrecy can lead to many challenges. I had many students with invisible disabilities who, because of their past experiences of being labeled and judged, decided not to disclose. Often this decision resulted in students not getting the accommodations and support they needed to succeed. When these students finally registered with disability services, it was because their parents forced them to or because they were having academic difficulties that put them on probation.

It took lots of convincing on my part for students to realize that they were entitled to accommodations, and that it was to their benefit to disclose their disability to their professors. I totally understood their hesitation. But my goal was to teach students that a disability is not what is bad, but rather, what is bad is trying to succeed in an educational environment that wasn't accessible for them because of their disability. What affected them was having to complete requirements where, because of their disability, they would struggle or not be able to do well. For instance, for someone with dyslexia, asking them to read is like asking me to walk, and typically, college courses do require reading. I encouraged students diagnosed with dyslexia to use accommodations, just like I use a wheelchair to get around. Because they had an invisible disability, they wanted to hold the diagnosis in secrecy, disagreeing with anyone who encouraged them to register for services. As a person with a visible disability, I never had to deal with this type of decision. People saw my disability whether I wanted them to or not. I only hoped that they would not make an immediate false judgment of my capabilities without getting to know me first.

Even with a physical disability, I often felt that my intelligence was questioned. No matter my successes and accolades, I was very aware of people's lack of comfort when interacting with me. It's as if people were walking on eggshells, not wanting to make a mistake and/or say the wrong thing. It was obvious that seeing my disability caused this lack of comfort. Not everyone behaved in this manner, though many did. It was refreshing when I noticed someone acting normally and without hesitation because of my disability. I appreciated it when I discovered that a person saw me beyond the wheels I was on.

I often have wondered where the discomfort with people with disabilities came from. I wonder if it is a result of fear. Are people afraid because individuals with disabilities are a reminder of what life could be like? Are people afraid of making mistakes? Do people lack exposure to differences? Regardless of the source, their discomfort really affected me. This was especially true when I was younger and strived to be liked by everyone. Now, I have come to realize that some people will never feel comfortable around me and that I shouldn't waste energy to try to have them see me differently. Discrimination against disability and other forms of diversity come from the same root.

I have learned a lot more about disability and the different types of effects it has on people since I married a man with a disability. Unlike me, Isidro became disabled as a teenager, whereas I became disabled as an infant. Isidro knew what life was like without a disability. I didn't, because, as far as I'm concerned, I have been disabled all my life. It became obvious that our viewpoints were different. This has helped me tremendously, because I learned from him that people do not have the right to be intrusive by asking about our disabilities before knowing us. He pointed out that I shouldn't give an explanation to people just to fulfill their curiosity. This was an important lesson for me to learn because I had always felt that I had to disclose my disability even to strangers. Professionally, this was also helpful for me to understand individuals who became disabled later in life and how this might mold their opinions about their condition.

My husband was diagnosed with juvenile rheumatoid arthritis as a teenager. Prior to this life-changing diagnosis, he had been the typical teen, working as a paperboy using his bicycle to deliver papers in his neighborhood, learning to play the guitar, and playing sports with his friends. Arthritis changed all of that. He was no longer able to ride a bike. Nor was he able to hold a guitar because of how his joints limited his range of motion. Likewise, he was no longer able to play sports because of his need to use crutches and because of his lack of flexibility.

Isidro's characteristics and the way he handled his disability are what led me to love him. I admired his fortitude and how he adjusted to his new situation with courage. I have always known my life as disabled, so I do not know what I am missing, but he does! I admired him because, even though his life changed dramatically, he didn't just stop living. He adjusted by finding tools to help him be independent and by relying on natural medicine to cope with the pain. He doesn't have the range of motion to bend down to put on his socks, yet he puts them on independently using a sock aid, which is basically a tube attached to a string. He rolls the sock on the tube and then using the string he throws it on the ground so that he can put his foot in the tube. He then pulls the string up so that the sock can slide onto his foot. He cannot shave or dress in the traditional way, but he manages his personal care independently. He has had multiple joints replaced but doesn't take any prescribed medication. He uses essential oils and supplements to help him manage any pain. Sometimes I say he is like the Six Million Dollar Man but without the millions. Or sometimes I tell him he is my Tin Man, but that he already has a heart.

I never thought I would get married because of my disability, much less thought that I would marry a person with a disability. But God had different plans and arranged so that I could meet my perfect life partner. It was our twenty-seventh anniversary on July 1, 2022. I am blessed to have married a person with a great desire, like mine, to progress and not let the disability dictate the trajectory of lives. We make a good couple, complementing each other in so many ways. Together we have built a good middle-class life. We maintain our small home, are busy out and about in society, raised two daughters with a grandchild on the way, and we have always overcome each obstacle united.

Because disability will affect every single person in life, I have three wishes. My first wish is that people would see disability not as bad, but just as a form of diversity. People with disabilities do not want to be pitied, much less ignored. We want to be a part of society by being included and understood. Second, I wish people would take the responsibility to do their part in providing accessibility. Often, access is an afterthought when it should be considered from the very beginning. Finally, my last wish is that people with disabilities, whether invisible or visible, would be offered the same opportunities in life. It is time that people with disabilities be fully integrated into society. The times of people with disabilities living in parents' basements, watching *Wheel of Fortune*, and waiting to collect a Social Security Disability check should be over. This requires all of us. Able-bodied persons' allyship is crucial.

Someday (hopefully far in the future), I will die, still being disabled. I'd like to be remembered as a person who didn't allow a disability to define me. I would like to be known as a person who lived a full life and who used her disability to advocate for inclusion for everyone, regardless of their diverse identities. I have had a great life, and if I were to ever be given the option to be reborn, I would choose to come back just as I am. I embrace my being fully and thank God for giving me so many attributes that erase much of the pain that I have suffered because of my disability.

REFLECTION QUESTIONS

1. How have you or someone close to you been affected by disability?
2. What are your attitudes about disability?
3. What can you do to be an ally and understand disability as a type of diversity?

CHAPTER 5

EFFORT

As a parent, I always remind my daughters that opportunities and success never come knocking on our doors. We must put in hard work and effort in finding them. No matter the dream, it will remain a dream if we do not put in the effort to make it a reality. Successful people are successful not because they are lucky or more intelligent. Most of the time, success is reached by people because of the amount of time, persistence, and effort put into the goal or project.

I used to believe that I was lucky. However, as I look back, each success I have had has been largely because of the effort I always put into anything I do. This is true for everything from the simple task of preparing dinner to any other goal I aimed to accomplish. I work hard. Things do not come easily. Every success I have had required my dedication and effort. I obtained an education despite the many barriers I encountered. I was organized and didn't waste time doing fruitless activities. I always saw my hard work and effort as an investment which I knew would be rewarded in the long run.

I knew the odds were against me because I came from a low-income status and because I had attended only schools for the disabled. I knew that I couldn't afford to fail. I navigated the complex environment of higher education all on my own. I became hyper focused on not wanting to fail. I did not procrastinate or find excuses for not exceeding any expectation I had for myself, and even the expectations others had of me. I was very successful, but it wasn't because of luck. I put aside any distractions, even when it prevented me from spending time with my family. My priority was each class and each assignment. I saw my effort in school as a step toward my goal. Perhaps my greatest motivation was that I thought that I couldn't work in menial jobs or get married.

I was equally successful in my thirty-year career as a faculty member at Harper College. I put effort into learning the job and staying up to date with my field. I put effort into supporting each student that I met. Any personal concern that may have been plaguing my mind was put aside so that I could focus on the student, the meeting, or the project. This resulted in receiving much recognition during my career, but more importantly for me, it helped my students reach their academic goals.

Effort is needed even for tasks that come out naturally because we are skilled. Logically, then, effort is even more important for difficult tasks where we lack skill. It is understandable that we want to avoid things that are difficult, but more effort is needed for what is challenging. No matter what, the assured outcome of lack of effort is failure. Even the most talented musicians practice and put in the effort. Olympic gold medal winners receive the recognition because of the effort they have placed on their sport.

More than once, I would encourage my students to use available resources such as the tutoring center, the math lab, and the library by explaining that these resources were for successful students who were putting in the effort to get the best grades possible. My students often admitted that they thought the services were only for students who were failing. They appreciated learning that the utilization of resources would not "out" them as students with disabilities. The reminder that "smart" students also use resources enlightened them to consider utilizing the available support services.

As complex human beings with varying skills and abilities, the amount of effort available to us can vary depending on what our strengths are.

For example, I find writing easy, so, although I do put in effort to get my thoughts down on paper, those with writing difficulties may have to put in much more effort. Similarly, I can probably figure out a complex algebraic problem, but the effort I would have to put into figuring it out would be greater than for someone who excels in math. Additionally, the amount of effort I put into gardening is probably higher than for those who do not have physical disabilities. Of course, there is a greater satisfaction in knowing that I have a beautiful garden *because* of the amount of effort I put into it. Knowing that we accomplish something because of our effort gives us great satisfaction.

However, we have often misinterpreted the Army recruitment slogan "Be All You Can Be" to mean that we can be whatever we want. This couldn't be farther from the truth. For instance, regardless of how much time and effort I would put into exercising my leg muscles, I would never be able to walk. I don't have the muscles to strengthen in the first place so, no matter the effort, I would never succeed in walking. Likewise, it was difficult for me to explain to students and their parents that sometimes, no matter the amount of effort, we cannot always accomplish what we want, especially when the goal may be unrealistic because of a disability.

Once, I wanted to demonstrate this concept to the students in one of my classes. I was a newer professional who wanted to support the students without discouraging them. When the students came into the classroom, I had the slogan "Be All You Can Be" written on the white board. I asked the students, "Do you believe we can be anything we want to be?" Most of the students were quick to defend their viewpoint that they could be anything they wanted to be if they put in the effort. I then pulled out a basketball I had brought to the classroom. I started to bounce the basketball. I said, "What if I told you I wanted to be the next Michael Jordan? Do you think I can do it? I would put in a lot of time and effort to be a good basketball player." I kept bouncing the ball as I waited for responses. With perplexed faces they were hesitant to respond. One student finally said "No. you can't. There are no women playing in professional basketball." Another student chimed in saying "No. You can't. You are too short." Interestingly after getting several responses, none of the students mentioned my disability as the reason I couldn't be the next Michael Jordan. I suspect that all of them likely had that on their minds. Perhaps they were afraid to offend me by pointing out my disability. I concluded the lesson by explaining that sometimes a disability can determine success in a field and that failure would not stem from a lack of effort.

Throughout my career I thought of other classroom activities to demonstrate that we cannot always be what we want to be, but that it doesn't mean that we can't be successful. I would share that, when I was their age, I wanted to be a lawyer because of my desire to make the lives of people with disabilities better. I went on to explain that, although I didn't become a lawyer, which was in great part due to my disability and lack of access at the law school, I had found a career where I still could work toward improving the lives of students with disabilities. Effort will not always result in getting what we want. However, effort *is* required in everything we succeed in. Sheer will won't make dreams come true.

I know that sometimes it may not be fair that someone can succeed with little effort, yet others may not regardless of how much effort is put in or how much they want it. Though this is true, students also learned that hard work and effort paid off most of the time. At the college, I often supported reverse transfer students. Reverse transfer students were students who had gone to a university but had not succeeded academically and were dismissed, forcing them to return home. They would transfer to Harper, their local community college, for assistance. I had a student, Lauren, who came to Harper unhappy about having been dismissed from the university she attended. She admitted that she failed at the university because she had not put in the effort. She used her time for social purposes, leaving little time to study for her classes. During our first appointments, we developed a plan to turn her situation around so that she could succeed. I motivated her by assuring her that if she worked hard, she might even be able to go back to the university. I said, "Lauren, once you taste success, you will never want anything else. However, success can only happen if you put in the effort." And that is exactly what she did. She ended up transferring back to the university and completing her degree. To this day, she remembers that conversation and she continues using it to meet her goals.

Lauren's younger brother, Paul, learned from his sister's mistakes and decided to start off at the community college and then transfer to a university of his choice. Paul had attention deficit disorder (ADD) and was very bright. He was a dedicated student who worked hard and put in the effort for each of his classes. He often quoted me, saying that Lauren had told him, "Once you taste success, you will not accept anything else." He completed his degree in two years, transferred to a university, and graduated two years later, proving that effort is rewarded.

Being a Latina helped me support the Latino students I worked with at the college. I know that culturally, we put priority on family and that we are quick to say "mañana." I know how we have been raised to live for the day. My parents were unique in that they wanted me to plan for my future. However, most of the time, as a Latina, I wanted immediate satisfaction and results. For some students, the thought of having to wait two or more years before getting a degree seemed impossible and not worthwhile. I was able to show them that living paycheck to paycheck was not a good way of life. I also explained that the more education they obtained, the higher their salary would be. I was able to make them understand that their education was a priority and that the bailes (dances) and other social activities could wait. I would motivate them to change their priorities, reminding them that the fun times with family and friends would always be there for them to enjoy.

I used my own personal experience by sharing how I navigated the opposing cultures of being Mexican while living in the United States. They couldn't believe it when I shared that when I attended law school, I would leave at 4 AM and not come back home until 10 PM to then do more studying. Additionally, they were shocked to learn that I held a full-time job while completing my master's degree and that sometimes, I would even stay overnight in a classroom so that I could have more time to study. I stressed that I did whatever it took and that I knew they could too. I often offered to talk to their parents if they questioned the amount of work required for a class, thinking that their students were out just having fun.

For example, a student named Tina accepted my offer and asked for an appointment so that I could talk to her parents. Her parents did not understand why she would come home so late. I met with Tina and her parents, and we had a great discussion about college life and all that it requires. Neither of the parents had gone to college, so they had no idea how college worked. They were shocked to learn that for each three-credit class, a student is required to study a minimum of two to three hours for each credit hour. I shared that it is for this reason that twelve credits or more is considered full-time. I calculated how outside-the-classroom work would take at least twenty-four to thirty-six hours a week, with classroom time being additional. It was important for the parents to know that their child would probably have to spend closer to thirty-six hours because their disability required additional time to use accommodations and resources. They often left the appointment enlightened, thanking me for explaining how much effort is a big component of success. Up to that point, they thought that the student would go to school a certain amount of time and then come home. It was foreign for them to know that sometimes the students would have to be on campus well after their classes were over.

I have always been an advocate for students with disabilities and Latino students. I know the sad statistics for both populations. College failure resulting in lack of completion and unemployment as well as underemployment rates tend to be much higher for these two populations. I tried to instill hope in them by urging them to work hard. I explained that it was important for them to get an education so that they could reach a position of power that would allow them to be part of the solution by sitting at the table where important decisions were made. I knew that more effort would be needed, but I also knew that this country needed their success.

My daughters also learned from a young age that unless there is an attempted effort, they will never know if they can succeed. When they were little, I got them involved in all sorts of activities, including baseball, karate, gymnastics, and learning to play an instrument. Ariana would often succeed with little effort whereas Ariel struggled more no matter how hard she worked. However, Ariel had a great personality and social skills, so I knew that would be helpful for her. Ariana was an introvert and struggled socially, so even when she was skilled in anything she attempted, it was difficult to convince her to focus on the activity. She avoided any activity that would require her to be in the spotlight or at the center of attention. Early on she demonstrated being a talented pianist, but she wanted lessons only with the condition that she would be allowed to do it for fun. She had no interest in doing recitals or piano contests. She took lessons and she put in the effort to improve her skills, even though she had the talent and playing the piano was easy for her. Both girls learned that hard work and effort were expected.

As parents with disabilities, we modeled how we could accomplish many things by working hard and giving dedicated effort, even when things were difficult because of our disabilities. With our respective disabilities, Isidro and I worked hard to provide for our family. We put in a lot of effort to give the girls a well-rounded experience by showing them that there were no excuses for not working toward achieving our goals. Even when Isidro and I experienced disability-related obstacles, we continued to work hard. I am certain that we could have used a multitude of excuses, one of them being pain, for not getting up each morning to go to work. However, we never did. We simply found solutions to get around our obstacles.

Our work ethic and our example of how effort pays off made both of my daughters stronger as individuals. They never resisted going to school and had perfect attendance most years, only missing if they were sick. They knew that they could not make an excuse for not putting effort, because we never did. This will be the greatest inheritance we will leave for them after we are gone. I believe my girls will remember the example we set forth as a motivator for them to persevere and strive to reach each one of their goals. Hard work and effort are essential to live this life. Those who do not put in the time and effort will not progress.

It is much easier to say, "I can't do it for X reason." Yes, it is hard work to put in effort. However, that is the only way. I see hard work as an investment in ourselves. It is the best investment with the highest interest return.

Each one of us is worth it. We have the capability to succeed when the goal is realistic and if success is wanted badly enough to put in whatever effort it takes. In this, every single person is on equal grounds. Effort is a great equalizer. This is how people with fewer resources can enter the door. If we want equity, we must first show that we are willing and ready to work hard and put in all the effort that is required. I know I have reaped the benefits of my hard work and I know the same is true for anyone who works hard. I never say I am lucky anymore. I worked for and earned my success.

REFLECTION QUESTIONS

1. What accomplishment(s) have you achieved because of your efforts?
2. Has your effort always been recognized? How or why not?
3. What have you done where your effort didn't make a difference?
4. Have you failed or not succeeded because of lack of effort? How?

CHAPTER 6
FAITH

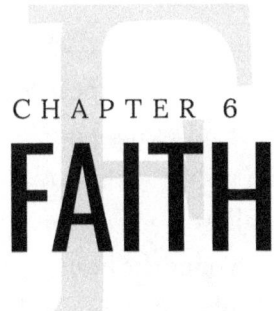

I AM NOT A RELIGIOUS PERSON, BUT I AM FAITHFUL. I WAS RAISED ROMAN Catholic and I continue to practice this religion. I say I am not religious because I do not spend endless amounts of time praying and going to masses. I pray the rosary with my family but do not pray it on my own. It is not that I do not see the value for the people who pray the rosary; it is more that I believe I practice my faith in a different way.

My faith has gotten me to the place I am today. I know that God makes everything possible. And though I sometimes get mad at God, I know that He is always present, and He always supports me. My parents taught me this. My mom had the greatest faith I have ever seen. She modeled faith in a way that I now practice. She was not one to always carry a rosary in her hands or to sit praying endless rehearsed prayers. She talked to God. She used her good deeds and hard work as prayer. I believe this is the type of faith I have.

Of course, I believe in God. How could I not? God's divine will is the only explanation for why I survived when I contracted polio and why I am here today. There was no medical treatment and no other type of intervention. I was in complete paralysis for six months, able only to breathe independently. All my mother could do was to pray and care for me in any way she could. I am certain that the couple of ounces of milk she fed me did not make a difference in my recovery. The true medicine was my mom's prayers and the fact that God listened to all her pleas. No scientific explanation exists.

Because of this miracle of life, I developed my own sense of faith. It was as if I felt that God allowed me to live because He had a purpose for me. I used this to always move forward no matter the suffering, pain, or obstacle. This allowed me to develop a closer relationship with God. I know He loves me without a single doubt. I know he allowed my disability because I was to be the instrument in teaching others about the beauty of life. My prayers are very similar to my mom's. I probably only know only a few of the established Catholic prayers. I don't have specific prayer times, although I guess I probably should. But mostly I just live every minute of my day with faith. My prayers are always rooted in gratitude. My main prayer is to always ask for strength to keep me going, no matter what obstacles are in front of me. As human as I am, I sometimes dwell in the pain, but as soon as I can, I move forward. I see each difficulty as a problem to solve and each day as an opportunity to support those around me. I try to be kind and love whomever I meet. I try to be the best wife and mother I can be. Again, I am human, so I know I sometimes fall short.

The only truth is that I believe. I believe that everything in this world has value and was placed lovingly by God. My faith makes me believe that God is perfect and doesn't make mistakes. Although some people may think that I should be mad or upset because of my disability, I am not. Do I allow worry and fear to enter my life? Yes, but I know that God always gives us the means to get through each obstacle. I am always amazed how God has His own plans, and though we may want to take control, everything happens the way God wants it and when He wants it. Each day we live is a miracle. We may think we know what will happen, but each day is a surprise. Sometimes beautiful, unexpected experiences happen that bring us joy.

Thanks to my education, I can understand the different viewpoints of faith. I respect each one of them. I simply choose to follow the faith that my parents taught me and modeled. In the end, I think that regardless of what a person believes, we are all inherently equal. I do believe that having faith makes life a bit easier, at least it has for me. I cannot see my life without faith and the assurance that what we do in this world matters. I don't know how I could get through the dark days of my life without faith.

Faith, to me, doesn't mean that I think God will provide me with each thing I say I need. I must just trust that He knows what's better for me than I do. So even with all my surgeries and broken bones, I believe they happened for a reason. Each experience has made me stronger, has made me stop taking everything for granted. As my physical condition continues to deteriorate with age, I have learned to appreciate what I can do independently today, knowing that it might well change tomorrow.

After gardening all day yesterday, this morning I woke up with severe back pain. My first prayer of the morning when I woke up was to say, "Thank you God for the many days I have had without back pain. Please help me with my back pain today." I am sure my prayer will be listened to, but if not, I know that God will be there to support me and help me find the best solution. In a nutshell, that is my faith.

Since my parents passed away, some of my siblings continue being practicing Catholics, going to church on Sundays, and praying. Some are not. However, I am sure that each one of us has faith and that the values my parents instilled in us continue being the motor that drives us. I know that whether they are practicing the faith or not, they still believe in God and would be right here to support me if I ever needed them.

Demonstrating faith differs for each person. My daughters inherited my faith, and both received the Catholic sacraments. As adults, they will make their own decisions. My daughters sometimes share their contrasting views regarding the Catholic faith. I am open to listening to them and respect their opinions. They are both very open to differences and believe that sometimes the doctrine is not open to all. I just listen and question them so that they make the best decision for themselves. Honestly, I am even open to changing my own mind if they share information that contradicts my beliefs. What is important to me is that they are good, kind, and loving young women who practice love and not hate.

My husband Isidro demonstrates faith differently than I do. I sometimes wish I'd see life through his faith lens. He listens to various ways that Christianity can be expressed. I tell him that I sometimes wish I could show faith as an innocent child like he does. He prays for everything, even what I consider trivial requests. For example, he often prays for sunny weather on a cloudy day. Somehow, my faith blocks me from making these types of requests. Perhaps I consider God too busy to worry about our weather. Yet, Isidro believes in his heart that if he asks God for anything, it will be granted. Additionally, he believes in signs as evidence that God is listening. I often hear him saying, "God is telling me that I shouldn't do this." Though he was raised Catholic, his view about life is like that of a child. Like a child who wants a particular toy for Christmas, Isidro wholeheartedly believes he will get what he asks for as well.

I believe in miracles but not in the way most people likely do. I do not believe that if I pray hard enough, I will someday wake up without a disability and be able to walk. Some people do believe that. Recently, on vacation, when Ariana and I stopped at an ice cream shop, this young girl, probably a high schooler, approached me and asked if she could pray for me. Ariana was surprised by the request because she had never been around when I had received similar requests in the past. The young girl said, "I just got baptized and I would love to pray for you. Would that be OK with you?" She looked so kind that I said yes, simply as a kind gesture for her. She held my hand, closed her eyes, and said, "Dear Jesus, you promised that whenever we pray in your name, you would hear our prayers. Please help this kind woman in the wheelchair so that she can walk again. Heal her from her infirmity. I pray this in the name of Jesus. Amen." She opened her eyes and said, "I know you will walk again."

I couldn't resist the opportunity for a teachable moment. I said, "Thank you very much for the prayer. I believe everyone needs prayers. I just want to tell you that I am fine without walking. I'd rather you pray for God to make me strong to handle living in an inaccessible world and to deal with people who say or do something that offends me. Also, I think there are so many other people who need your prayers more than I do. Again, thank you." She looked at me and didn't know what to say. We ended up not buying ice cream, not because of the prayer, but because we discovered it was frozen yogurt and we wanted the real thing.

When we got back into our van, Ariana looked at me and said, "Boy, that was strange! Why did she want to pray only for you? Doesn't she know I may need prayers too?" I told her, "Because her lens allowed her only to see my disability as something that needed to be cured. She didn't see me as a human being that, like everyone else, was just looking for ice cream." Ariana then asked, "Do you think she really believes you will be able to walk?" I said, "Well, faith moves mountains, but I am not sure if it will move my legs."

We cling to faith anyway we can. It allows painful experiences to seem more bearable. Yet there are some atheists or agnostics who do not believe in a higher being. I respect their viewpoint, though I don't understand how they could live life not believing in God. I know I couldn't live without the presence of my faith. It is what grounds me and makes me move when I just want to give up. It is the hope that I am serving a purpose and that what I choose to do daily makes a difference. It is my desire to love others regardless of who they are.

Sometimes I have silly thoughts. I have thought, "What if I am wrong in believing there is a heaven and that I should strive to get there? What if, after I die, there is nothing?" I have had these questions multiple times, and my answer is always the same. I am happier believing that there is a higher being. If I am wrong, at least my life was better on earth. The bottom line is that we will not know the truth until our lives end. It's OK for me not to know the truth for a long while!

Another silly thought I have had is "If heaven is so good, shouldn't I want to get there sooner rather than later? Why should I eat healthy food then?" Of course, this question often comes after the guilt of having eaten an unhealthy, usually sweet, treat. The answer is always the same. We should strive to live our very best lives on earth because, in the end, that is what will determine if we get to heaven or not. The bottom line is that there are many unexplainable questions. But faith is living life as well as possible because of the belief that there is more than just this life. My belief that Jesus came to earth as a human and died for us brings me comfort in my days of suffering. Faith is believing without having the absolute confirmation of what is to come.

Another negative thought I sometimes have is "If there is a God, why does He allow war, famine, mass shootings, and pain?" I know this is a question I have heard from nonbelievers. I am not sure if I will ever know why. I plan to ask Him when I get to heaven. What I do know is that in God's perfection, He created us all good, but that in our humanness, we are the ones who allow evil and hate to enter our hearts. With evil and hate, we hate others instead of loving them; we want riches, instead of sharing what we have; we are self-righteous instead of celebrating the differences in others. He allows us to make our own decisions by giving us free will, and even with all our mistakes, He is there to love us and support us through everything. He is so loving that he will forgive us for everything, especially when we repent.

The only certain thing is that we were all born and that we will all die. Having faith allows me to understand that truth. What sense would it make to strive to be good and avoid doing harm if there was nothing afterward? To me it doesn't make sense. This is especially comforting when we lose a loved one. When my mom died, doubts came to my mind that prolonged my suffering. All I ever wanted was for my mom to be well. I knew that she was well if I was well. This was in big part why I continued going forward even when I was suffering. When she died, I wanted some assurance that she was OK. I lost many nights of sleep thinking that she may not be well.

I didn't regain my peace until I used the faith she taught me. She taught me to believe that there is a heaven. This made me feel better because I knew she was in heaven, and that although she was no longer with me, she would always be watching me. I began envisioning her in the most beautiful garden, which brought me serenity in my pain. I have not seen signs of her presence, but I know she is always with me. Sometimes a memory will come that reminds me that she is constantly supporting me. In my garden, she is always with me.

For me, faith has made my life possible. My mom's faith brought me back to life after she was given no hope. Faith continues to give me strength, and because of it, I am prepared for whatever is in store in my future. I depend on it as much as I depend on breathing. I would cease to exist without it, and my life would certainly be meaningless without my faith.

I recognize that, in many instances in my life, it was difficult to maintain faith. I couldn't explain why God allowed me to suffer, and I thought it was unfair that I had to endure the pain I was feeling. At times I was so mad that I would revolt and tell myself, "God doesn't exist!" I would be angry and continue, "If God existed, He wouldn't allow this to happen to me when I work so hard, never give up, and help everyone I can." However, when I was angry with God, I felt lost and alone. I felt as if I couldn't go on. I realized that God is who gives me strength, and I acknowledged that many other good people I know suffered even more. I felt selfish and self-absorbed.

This realization is what motivated me to become an advocate and give back to my community. I discovered that my pain lessened when I wasn't just thinking of myself. I found ways to focus on others. I worked harder in supporting students, especially those who I knew suffered more than I ever did. I felt most happy when I knew that others were happy because of something I did. My faith was more solidified with each student who taught me a lesson. Each student, in their own way, helped me grow personally. I was certain that I was living my mission in life working with them.

I also got involved with Life Directions, an organization that focuses on teaching at-risk young adults to become responsible for their lives. I found that the more I focused on others, the less I hurt in my own life. Though I was giving my time, I was the one receiving the benefit. I loved working closely with Father John and Sister Rosalie, both very kind, who focused on giving rather than receiving. With Father John's spiritual direction, my faith grew. I learned that I was giving myself too much importance and that by helping others I would be helping myself. For over thirty years I have been affiliated with Life Directions. I see it as an important reminder that faith *does* move mountains, as evidenced by the many young adults Life Direction supports who turn their lives around for the better.

Life is complex. We need all the support we can to live it. Faith is the lifeline I need to navigate the muddy waters that I sometimes face. I have shared my faith, but I know there are different ways to be faithful and spiritual. I believe we each need to find the source of support that will get us through each day. I guarantee that with support we will discover how beautiful life can be.

REFLECTION QUESTIONS

1. Do you consider yourself a faithful person? Why or why not?
2. What is an example of a time when your faith helped you through difficulties?
3. What do you do or use to get through your difficulties?
4. How does faith or lack of faith affect your life?

CHAPTER 7

GRATITUDE

My greatest attribute as a human being is that I am very grateful for all my blessings. I am very blessed in every aspect of my life. First and foremost, I am grateful for my life. A diagnosis of polio, and the effects it had on me, threatened my life, yet I survived because of my parents' faith and the sacrifices they made in working toward what was best for our family. Above all, this happened because of God's mercy. I am grateful that I woke up from my complete paralysis because the life I have had has been marvelous.

Throughout my hardships, I always remembered that I could have died, but I didn't. I was taught by my parents not to take anything for granted because my life could be worse and that life was a miracle. Instead of focusing on what I didn't have, they insisted that I focus on all that I did have. This moral lesson always helped me to quickly shift away from self-pity and to acknowledge how fortunate I am. Instead of focusing on a broken bone or being in a wheelchair, I quickly realized that I was lucky to be a part of the most loving family and to be in a country where I received the best medical care and education. I always kept in mind that there were others in much worse situations.

I used to get annoyed when my mother wouldn't allow me to complain. She would stop me immediately, reminding me that I had no reason to complain when I lived in a loving family, had a roof over my head, and had plenty of food on the table. I was annoyed because I didn't want to think about the worst life situations; I preferred to compare my life to those without disabilities who were otherwise, in my opinion, better off than me. I sometimes wished that my mom would empathize with me when I was feeling sorry for myself, but as I grew, I realized that what I was really seeking was sympathy and not empathy. There is a big difference between both, though at the time I didn't know it. My mom empathized with me by understanding my struggles, knowing how much I suffered. However, by no means did she feel sympathy for me, because that would have meant that she felt sorry for me. But she didn't. With empathy there is an understanding of another's pain, but with sympathy there is pity. My mom was just grateful I was alive, since everyone had told her I'd die because of polio. There was no room for any pity, and she never condoned me feeling it either.

I modeled this same point of view as I raised my family. In my daily life I taught my girls an understanding that it was important to help the family because it was their responsibility as members of that family. They learned that helping was not because Isidro and I were to be pitied; as children, they learned that they had to help around the house but also knew that both Isidro and I were very capable. They were grateful for having us as parents, even with all our limitations. They appreciated how we provided for their every need. Others in the public didn't understand our family dynamics and sometimes interjected their opinions about how our family operated. The comments made by others stemmed from viewing us through the lens of pity.

My girls were often confused by the commentary made when we were out shopping. One time, while checking out of a grocery store, in my presence, the cashier told Ariana, "You are so nice to be helping the disabled lady. Does she pay you?" Ariana was about ten years old and for good reason got confused by the comment and question. On the way home we discussed the incident. First, I pointed out that the cashier never even considered the possibility that I could be her mom. Second, the cashier didn't even see me, ignoring me as a human and only seeing my disability, assuming that I was incapable of doing anything on my own. And third, she was operating from a pitying point of view, negating the possibility that Ariana was just being a member of a supportive family.

My girls never considered the support they gave us as "helping" but rather saw it as a responsibility as being a part of a loving family. They were grateful for all we did for them. They knew we worked hard, so they never had to worry about asking for things they needed. We enjoyed our time together as a family and really appreciated our long road trips and vacations to different parts of the country. They were grateful for being a part of a family where there was peace and harmony. Sure, they could have easily been resentful about being raised by two parents with disabilities and having responsibilities that other girls their age didn't. For a long time, I worried about this. However, I shouldn't have worried, because they chose to be grateful instead. They focused on the positive instead of the negative.

When they were little, we were quite the sight. I would push a double stroller while in my wheelchair. It was inevitable that people would stop in their tracks to stare at us. I had to quickly develop a strategy to help the girls better process how others saw us. Every time someone would stare, either while shopping or getting out of our van when we arrived at our destination, I would say, "Oh look. They are watching us, wishing they had our nice van with a ramp. We are so blessed to have the van because many people cannot afford to buy one." I redirected their thoughts to think positively instead of negatively. This helped them to be grateful instead of focusing on feeling sorry for our family.

We all have reasons to be grateful. It is a matter of acknowledging that there are so many others who are suffering in ways we can't even imagine. For some reason, even though we all want the good, when we have it good, we don't appreciate it. Perhaps because I'm aging and am having more physical limitations than before, I am constantly reminded that everything could always be worse. During tough times, I want to remember that. I want to appreciate each day that I live, especially when it is pain free.

Sure, there are people who can walk, people who are richer, people who are smarter, people who have more talents, people who . . . fill in the blank. However, there are also people who can't even sit in a wheelchair, people who are poor and hungry, people who are ignorant of spirit, and people who have talents and don't use them. Focusing on the grass that is greener on the other side doesn't let us appreciate our own grass. Being grateful for what we have brings more joy to our lives.

I've mentioned that I have recently started gardening to be closer to my mom who loved gardening. This newfound hobby has opened my eyes to nature's beauty, which I had always taken for granted. I now notice the birds singing, the butterflies flying, and even the pesky squirrels that dig into my plants. I have a new appreciation for God's beautiful creation and a love for all that lives. Everyone can look around and find something they hadn't noticed before. This new discovery may fill their hearts with gratitude just like it filled mine.

My dad was a good role model in noticing nature and being grateful for the simplest of things. He would often say, "I am so blessed that I can see this beautiful day." We would regularly say, "I am so blessed because I can eat whatever I want." Or he would say, "I am so grateful that God gave me such a beautiful family. I am the richest man alive." He never complained about the fact that he never went to school or that he had to work in factories to support his huge family. He never complained about any financial limitation, not being able to drive, not speaking English well enough, not traveling or taking vacations, etc. How often do we complain without looking at what we do have?

I became good at being grateful perhaps because I was so often exposed to others who suffered more. I went to school with students who had all kinds of disabilities. I appreciated my independence when I noticed that some of my classmates were not able to feed themselves. I appreciated my ability to use my arms when I noticed that some students didn't even have arms to use. I appreciated my sight when I noticed that there were students who couldn't see. If each of us looks deep within, we will discover all of our different privileges.

My field of education also exposed me to people who had tough lives. I've worked with many students, all with disabilities, some more severe than others. Finding out how some students lacked a supportive family and lived in abusive households made me appreciate my own family and the safety it provided. Some students were undocumented and could not apply for financial aid or many scholarships, which made them to have to work hard to pay for their own educations. One such student, Jose, worked two jobs to take two classes that he had to pay for entirely on his own. He finished his law enforcement degree and then started his bachelor's degree. I remember a conversation I had with him. He said, "Pascuala, is it worth the effort to get a degree when I know that without a social security card, I will never be hired to be a cop?" My response was, "How do you like what you are learning?" He immediately said, "Oh, I love it. I enjoy all my law enforcement classes." I then said, "Well, there you have it. You are working hard to pay for your classes, and you enjoy the satisfaction of your effort. We do not know the future. Immigration laws may change. But even if they don't, no one can take away your knowledge, and trust me that, with hard work, you will someday find the path."

This conversation with Jose made me grateful for becoming a United States citizen, which was made possible because of my parents' sacrifices to bring us to Chicago documented, so that we could have a better life. Immigration was easier in the '70s, which allowed my dad to get residency for the entire family. Now, undocumented students do not have the advantage that my family had. There are stricter rules, and it takes a long time to get residency even with a lawyer involved. What is sad is that Jose came to Chicago when he was two years old. All he knows is the United States, yet he cannot have all the benefits of living in this country.

Some students I worked with had severe cognitive difficulties and read no higher than a third grade level. Many had a lot of ambition to do well, and some succeeded with the right support and opportunities. Others didn't. This often reminded me to be grateful for my ability to read and write. I may not be able to walk, but I am a quick learner who can speak, read, and write in two languages. There are many other examples that, in one way or another, led me to be grateful for what I have.

My involvement with social justice activism also taught me to appreciate the freedom and privileges I have in this country. I not only met many other activists who were in the fight for greater reasons than me, but I also appreciated our freedom to publicly participate in activist rallies where we advocated for changes that could make our country better for citizens with disabilities. I was grateful and acknowledged that I could do everything on my own except for walking. During protests, I observed that there were so many activists who depended on someone else to eat, go to the bathroom, or take their medication. Many of the individuals who protested alongside me lived in nursing homes because family members couldn't care for them due to their disabilities. There were others whose disabilities impeded their ability to communicate. I was grateful for being able to care for myself and for my ability to communicate not just in one language, but two.

I am sure that readers who reflect on all they possess will also come up with a long list of reasons to be grateful. It is all up to us to shift our thinking. When we take the time to reflect, we can learn to stop focusing on what is not going well and instead appreciate all that we do have. I know that our lives can be difficult, but by simply nurturing our thoughts and training our minds to be grateful, the burdens are likely to be reduced. Like a good plant, we must harvest and tend to our thinking. Every single person can find something to be grateful for in life.

Although I believe I am a grateful person, I know others who are even more grateful and who are models for me to follow. I have a cousin who exemplifies what gratitude should really look like. Lucia has been battling a difficult disease that impacts all her organs. She can no longer walk. She must be fed intravenously. Her life is constantly threatened, having to enter the hospital regularly with little hopes of survival. And to make things worse, my cousin, her father, who is one of Lucia's caregivers, recently got diagnosed with cancer.

What is amazing is that every time I contact Lucia, mostly via text, she is there to offer me support, wanting to focus on me. She never complains about her conditions. She continues to have high hopes for the future, and her faith is beyond anything I will ever comprehend. I look up to her. Every time I begin my well-known route to self-pity, I quickly remember her. I am then quickly able to recognize and appreciate all that I have, because it helps me see that whatever is bothering me is trivial. I know she is in this world to touch lives. I am grateful she has touched mine.

Other people are always going through very difficult hardships, but we tend to focus only on our own issues, as if no one else is suffering. I know I always question God and ask him "why?" However, I am trying to not just go to God when things are not well. I want to constantly thank him for all that I have, which is a lot, and probably more than I will ever deserve.

I am getting better and better at being grateful. This past Thanksgiving, as we prepared to eat our bountiful dinner, we went around the table and expressed what we were thankful for during that year. When it was my turn, I said, "This has been a great year! I wrote and published two books; Isidro and I are keeping busy with the promotion of my two books; Ariel is engaged to a nice young man; Ariana is about to finish college; and we have survived the pandemic." My husband looked at me with incredulous eyes. He stated, "What about your two broken bones and being bedridden for almost the entire summer?" Laughing I said, "I guess all the blessings erased all the bad from my mind, so I am just grateful."

I am so grateful for all my blessings but especially for the people I have in my life to support me. I am so fortunate to have a huge family, ranging from my husband and daughters to my siblings, their spouses, and all their families. There are over eighty-three people in my immediate family, not even counting aunts, uncles, or cousins. I am also grateful for always having friends who I've met through my life's journey. I try to show my gratitude by demonstrating in simple ways how much they are appreciated. I don't ever take their love and support for granted. Their unconditional love never goes unnoticed.

I also can't help but to be thankful for strangers. Yes, I could focus on those whose ignorant comments may hurt me, but I'd rather focus on so many kind people in the world. I'd like to believe that people are kind until they prove me wrong. I try to be friendly and genuinely love people. I am grateful for the opportunity I get to converse and learn from others. I can connect with people because with each interaction I grow as a person.

Sometimes the kindness of strangers surprises me. On more than one occasion, I have had people in my church approach me to give me gifts. One woman would give me the sign of peace then hand me a $100 bill during Christmas and Easter. I am not sure if she did it because she felt I needed it because of my disability, but I gratefully received her gift and then passed it forward for someone else in need. Another couple who were also parishioners of my church bought tickets for my family to attend the Christmas dinner, saying that they wanted to get to know us better. The kindness of others is always appreciated.

With any struggle, I have my share of support. I jokingly say that when something good or bad happens in my life, I must share it immediately with at least seven family members or friends. I like to celebrate my happy moments and I want to be consoled during my difficult times also. I'd like to believe that family and friends would also reach out to me for support and encouragement. After all, friends are the family we choose.

Some of the kindness I receive is unearned and perhaps because of God's divine intervention. There have been many times where I have been in the right place at the right time. It amazes me how God helps me by putting kind people in my life. My first book, *Not Always a Valley of Tears*, has connected me to so many people that I would have otherwise not connected with in life. There is my friend Linda, who connected with me after over a decade of not seeing each other. She is now a very important person in my life because of her unconditional support, her invaluable knowledge, her multitude of connections, and her overall big heart. I am grateful that I have her as a friend and support.

Likewise, without seeking it, I receive opportunities that result in the best types of experiences. After writing the memoir, I knew I also wanted it to be available as an audiobook because I wanted the book to be accessible for all readers, including those with visual impairments. I didn't know where to begin to get it recorded, especially because I wanted to record it in my own voice. Again, somehow it happened. I met a kind librarian who not only encouraged me to enter my Spanish memoir in a contest (which I won) but also advocated for and facilitated my using the library's recording studio even though I do not live in that library's community. So not only did I get the English and Spanish book recorded, but I also gained great friends, the librarian and my audio editor. Life has been good to me all the time. All the time, life is good to me.

I work hard and always take the opportunities I am offered. I am thankful that the opportunities are there and that I most always say "yes." The rest becomes just another blessing to show me that I have so many things to be grateful for in my life. Those who take the time to reflect and analyze their own blessings will come to the same conclusion. Life is full of events, experiences, surprises, and people who give us reasons to be grateful. Sometimes, the only two words on my mind are "thank you!" Everything else, including our suffering, pain, and struggles disappear because they stop mattering when we have a grateful heart. Do me a favor and acknowledge all the blessings in your life and be grateful for them.

REFLECTION QUESTIONS

1. When do you take the time to list what you are grateful for in your life?
2. Do you consider yourself to be a grateful person; why or why not?
3. How has the practice of gratitude helped your life?
4. What can you do to practice being grateful in your life?

CHAPTER 8
HUMOR

LAUGHING IS ALWAYS BETTER THAN CRYING! I HAVE USED THIS PHILOSO-phy regularly throughout my life. Painful incidents turn into funny situa-tions when we see them through the lens of humor. I prefer laughter over pain and tears any day. I hope everyone else does, too. We must laugh at ourselves to lighten any burden on our shoulders. Many times, I have turned painful experiences into experiences I can smile at, simply by using humor.

We shouldn't always take life so seriously. When we do, we are invit-ing resentment, self-pity, envy, and pain into our lives. Again, it is up to us. Sometimes people feel like they need permission to lighten a situation with humor. But I have always been one who welcomes humor, and nine out of ten times, what could have been a painful experience turns out to be funny. I have had many humorous friends who had the ability to make my falls, when I walked on crutches, into a joke. Of course, they first made sure I was not hurt. I now remember those falls, but not because of the embarrassment or even the pain, but because of how funny the situation was. Falling and then having a friend sing "If you're happy and you know it, kiss the floor" seriously changed the embarrassing fall into something more positive. Additionally, after my ordeal last summer when I broke two bones, we looked back and laughed saying, "The ambulance arrived before the pizza."

My friends have said that I am a funny lady. I know that my friends always laugh at my craziness. In my great desire for independence, I sometimes get myself in tough situations. One example quickly comes to mind. When I worked at Harper as a faculty member, I entered the Program for Achieving Student Success (PASS), which I developed and coordinated, into a contest. We were notified that we had won the award, and I was invited to receive the recognition in Boston. My boss Tom could not attend. I couldn't pass up the opportunity, so I traveled to Boston by myself. After receiving the award early one morning, I still had the rest of the day before I had to fly back to Chicago. I have always loved swimming so I went to check out the pool. As I expected, they had no lift. But I really, really, wanted to go swimming. So, I told myself, "How hard can it be? There are steps I can use to get out." I knew getting in was a piece of cake. All I had to do was to plunge in. (Gravity sometimes is a wonderful thing.) So I went to change in my room and quickly returned to the pool.

As I predicted, there was no problem getting in. I swam back and forth, loving that I was the only person in the pool. I swam for close to an hour, then got tired enough that I was ready to get out. I had left my wheelchair close to the pool's steps, thinking I'd be able to get out by scooting up each step and then into my wheelchair. Well, it was easier said than done. I tried every which way I could without success. I did not have the necessary arm strength to pull myself out. I then turned my brain into problem solving mode, thinking of all possible solutions. I questioned, "Should I yell HELP?" And quickly reasoned, "No, that wouldn't work." I then looked at my wheelchair and remembered I had left my phone on it. I was able to reach my phone, being careful to not drop it in the water. I asked myself, "Who should I call? Should I call 911?" I played the scenario in my head and opted not to do that. I then remembered that I had the hotel's number on my recent calls. I chose to call the front desk and ask for help.

That conversation was hilarious! I said, "I am one of your guests, and I need help getting out of the pool." Confused, the friendly woman asked,

"You need what?" I repeated my need, but I included additional details. I responded, "I am one of your guests. I use a wheelchair. I came swimming and now I cannot get out of your pool." The woman took a few seconds to process what I had said, and then responded, "Oh. I see. I will send someone to help." I then put my phone back on my chair and swam a few more minutes while waiting for the rescue.

A few minutes later, two Latino men, dressed in their hotel uniforms, showed up. They looked confused, like they weren't sure why they had been sent to the pool. I asked, "Hablan en Español?" Both responded "Si." I then explained the situation, and I could almost hear their minds working as they tried to find a way to address the issue. Without telling me, one of the men took off his shoes and socks and told the other man, "Voy a ir por dentro y tu jálala" (I am going to go in, and you pull her). The man rolled up his pants and came down the steps. To be honest, rolling up his pants ended up not mattering. He was soaked! After several attempts and with a lot of trepidation, they managed to get me out.

Once on my chair, after thanking them, I went back to my room. Negative thoughts started to come to my mind. I started to feel sorry for myself, telling myself that I couldn't do anything and that I should be embarrassed of myself. However, I also began thinking about how worried the men looked. I began laughing even more when I visualized the man with his rolled-up pants getting all wet. It was funny! I allowed myself to laugh about it and quickly got rid of the negative thoughts I started to have. Humor changed the situation, and instead of feeling bad, I found it humorous.

I should probably stay out of pools, but I love swimming too much. I advocated for Harper to put a lift into their pools so that I and other students with disabilities could access it. I registered for an aquacise course that was taught by a colleague friend. We chatted a bit, and I explained that I would do my own exercises since it was unlikely I would be able to do the exercises she had planned.

The lift was dusty because of lack of usage after being locked up in a closet, but I celebrated when I was able to use it to get into the pool. I probably shouldn't have celebrated so fast, though, because after the class was over and

I tried to get out, the lift stopped functioning. It didn't want to work to lift me out of the pool. The teacher, who had stayed out of the pool throughout the class, began panicking. She jumped in to see if she could get the lift to work again. She couldn't. She then said, "I am going to get out to see who I can call for help." When I saw two firemen come, I figured she had called 911. I wondered if she used the famous line "She's fallen and she can't get up." The firemen had no problems pulling me out. Again, I had two options, but I decided to laugh at the situation that could have made me cry. And as a bonus, that teacher and I developed a strong relationship after that experience.

I wish I could say that now that I am older, I have stopped doing crazy things. No chance. Recently, I got myself into another hilarious predicament. I saw the weekly sale paper that comes to our house and was thrilled to see that the bottles of Coke were on sale at a nearby grocery store. I told Isidro, "Let's go to buy some Coke. They have four six-packs of twenty-ounce bottles of Coke for $10. We can't beat that." Isidro typically follows along with me, so we went for the sale. Because he uses crutches, if we go to the store for something quick, he usually drives and stays in the van while I go in on my own to quickly get what we need. My wheelchair can zoom pretty quickly.

I went straight to the beverage's aisle. I found the Coke bottles fast. Because I cannot push a cart with my wheelchair, I had to figure out how to carry twenty-four bottles of Coke on my lap. I was determined. I put the six packs anywhere I could, using my lap, underarms, and even my boobs to try to secure the sodas so they wouldn't fall off, since I knew I would not be able to pick them up if they did. Prior to the pandemic, other shoppers always offered help, but not anymore. I imagine it's because people are concerned about COVID. I barely could move, but I got to the check-out aisle. I could see the cashier smirk, probably judging me as the "crazy lady in the wheelchair on coke that loves Coke." Luckily, she only asked for one of the items on the belt to scan the price. I was glad, because I had finally found the perfect way to hold all four six-packs. Of course, I still had to figure out a way to get them in the van. Once I did, I felt I needed to celebrate! It was so satisfying to accomplish what I wanted to do, even if it was silly! I still laugh each time I drink a bottle of Coke.

After this experience, I finally wanted to resolve my problem with grocery carts. I went to Walgreens and saw that they had small rolling baskets there. I told myself, "This would be perfect, so I won't struggle carrying groceries." I decided to look online and found a warehouse nearby that sold similar carts. Again, Isidro went with me on my crazy treasure hunt. Because there was one tiny step to get into the warehouse, Isidro had to be the one to get out of the van this time. He went in, and soon after called me saying, "Cuali, they are distributors for stores, and they will only sell packs of six carts, but they can engrave them." I said, "That won't work. I just need one. Ask them if they'd sell just one." Because Isidro had me on speaker phone, I overheard the man say, "I can't do that."

I asked Isidro to put the man on the phone. In a sweet voice, I said, "Can you please make the exception? I am in a wheelchair and the basket on wheels would help me tremendously. It is hard for me to push a regular cart, and not all stores have rolling baskets." My husband chimed in, saying, "She couldn't even enter the warehouse because of a step. Did you know that is a violation of the ADA?" Quickly, the man responded by being more flexible. He said, "OK, but you will have to pay the cost for the one basket, which is $29.99. But I will even throw in a mesh bag for your trouble." I said, "Deal." I bet that Isidro mentioning the ADA violation helped in changing his mind. To prevent people from thinking I stole the cart, I now carry the receipt in my purse.

Humor adds spice to life. It has the potential to turn a difficult situation into a positive, memorable experience. But we must be open to it because it is a sure way to make life less difficult and more colorful. We must laugh at ourselves and help others to find the sunshine in an otherwise stormy event. Any time I allow myself to laugh, I transform what is happening from misery to joy.

Humor can be used even in the most serious situations. I have used humor to help students, which taught them how to look at things differently, often converting a depressing feeling into hope. Anna was a student who needed a service animal. She got approved to use her dog, Tubby, on campus. Although she had the documents to support her accommodation request, after several visits to my office, I had my doubts about Tubby having the skills to be a service animal. Tubby, a beautiful German Shepherd, did everything except what Anna asked her to do. It was obvious that Tubby was not trained and probably served more as a therapy dog. However, because Anna provided the necessary documentation, I had no other option but to approve her accommodation request.

One day, when I was giving Anna a tour of the campus, we ran into a group of the college's administrators, who were apparently all leaving a meeting together. This was too much stimulus for Tubby, and when Anna was distracted, she let go of the leash and Tubby took off running. Anna and I were both in wheelchairs, so we zoomed after Tubby to try to trap her. The group of administrators did not know what to do except watch. All of them were frozen and no one helped. Finally, we got Tubby back under Anna's control. When we went back to my office, we laughed, imagining what the administrators might have been thinking. Anna and I strategized on how to prevent that situation from happening again. Laughing lightened the conversation and as a result Anna was not as defensive when we talked about Tubby's lack of training.

Sometimes what was said in my office was so funny that when I shared it with my colleagues, they thought I must have been making it up. For example, I shared that a student had blatantly said that he hated Mexicans. His diagnosis was Autism, so I took his comment lightly. I found it funny that he had told a Mexican that he hated them. If I took things too seriously, I would have ended up insulted and would have made a big deal out of an innocent occurrence where he obviously didn't intend to hurt me. The student was just voicing his frustration over not being able to understand his boss at a restaurant who primarily spoke Spanish to his employees.

Our jobs as disability service providers were difficult. My colleagues and I used humor to help us through tough situations. To get through a rough semester, we'd support each other, laughing away our stress. To do this type of work, humor is essential. I believe this is true for any job, but even more so for working with students with disabilities. We never laughed at students, but we did laugh at some of the things they said and shared. How can laughter be avoided when one of my students shared that she needed a strapless bra and so she used coffee filters instead of buying the bra? We sometimes must give ourselves permission to laugh.

One of the funniest experiences was with a student who not only had learning disabilities but also seemed quite immature. She would bring birthday treats for each birthday and made sure to dress up for Halloween. This should have been a clue for me. One time, while working with Angela, she seemed more distracted than usual. I asked, "Angela, is something bothering you?" She looked at me and responded, "I am worried. I think I may be pregnant. I haven't gotten my period and it's a week late." I said, "Well, sometimes periods are delayed especially when there is stress. Could that be it?" She nodded no. I continued, "We can go to health services, and you can quickly take a pregnancy test so that you can know for sure. It is confidential and it is free. If you want, I can go with you." She smiled, and responded, "Yes, please."

We went to the building where the office of health services was located, and I had her sign in. Within minutes, the nurse came out to get Angela, and I was told that I should wait outside. Not even five minutes later, they both came out. Perplexed, I wondered if they got the results that quickly. The nurse said, "You are all done, Angela. Pascuala, Angela gave me permission to talk to you; can you come back for a minute?" "Of course," I said.

The nurse looked at me with questioning eyes. Hesitantly, she questioned, "Why did you think that she was pregnant and that she should have a test?" Confused, I responded, "Well, she was anxious because she had missed a period, and I thought it would help her to know if, indeed, she was pregnant." In a giggle, she said, "By chance, did you ask her when she last had sex?" I admitted that I hadn't, but retorted, "I assumed she recently had sex if she had the suspicion that she was pregnant." Still with a smirk on her face she said, "Well, she says she is a virgin because she is Jewish, and her mom would kill her if she had sex." I couldn't believe what I was hearing. I couldn't stop laughing at myself for not asking the obvious question. Joining her in her laughter, I said, "Thank you. I think I will have a talk with her about the birds and the bees and will add this to my job description. From now on, I will not assume anything about any of my students and will just ask them direct questions even if they seem silly to me."

At home, I live with two introverts, my daughter Ariana and my husband Isidro. Though introverts, they do like to have a good time, so we are constantly teasing each other. When we went on vacation to Branson, Missouri, recently, the bed was too high for me to transfer, and we didn't want to repeat my fall in California that resulted in broken bones because the bed had been too high. I wasn't going to take the risk to try to get into bed without help. When we called the front desk to see if they could lower the bed and was told no, we began strategizing on how I could get into the bed safely. We laughed at all the possible solutions we jokingly found. I came up with using a crane or Ariana pulling me with a rope. Though it was a serious concern, our laughter took away my anger for not having adequate access that could possibly result in another injury.

Similarly, when we saw that the faucet in the walk-in shower was at least four feet away from the shower seat I'd be using, we began to think about silly solutions. One idea I had was to do stretching exercises so that my arms could get at least two feet longer. Of course, Ariana ended up being the solution. When I got into the shower, I'd call her to turn on the faucet. The first time, my skin almost peeled because of how hot the water was, since we'd had to estimate where the warm water was on the faucet. Ariana laughed as I told her how I'd just sprinkle a little bit of water at a time so that I wouldn't burn up.

Humor changes our mindset. Anger turns into laughter. Fear turns into courage. Depression turns into joy. I am sure we can all think about funny things that happen all the time. Of course, sometimes the laughter comes later and is not immediate. When we are in a stressful situation, we might be acting irrationally, so we may not be able to see the humor. However, once the issue or situation is over, we sometimes look back and laugh.

We have two cats, Charlie and Rosie, who have been members of our family for eight years. When Ariel moved out, she bought a beautiful dog, a mini-Australian Shepherd named Luna. A few months after moving out, she decided to return home, dog and all. Charlie and Rosie were less than happy. Charlie decided to escape, even though both cats had been raised as domestic cats. Ariana imagined Charlie saying, "Hell no. I can't live with a cat *and* a dog. I am out of here!" When this happened, we were all devastated and searched for Charlie endlessly. We posted signs around the neighborhood, announcing a reward for assistance in finding him. We even left him food in our yard, hoping he'd return.

Because he was not microchipped, we lost hope. But after he had been gone for several days, I went out to the yard and heard meowing. I couldn't believe that he had returned. Charlie is a beautiful long-haired white cat, but when he returned, he was brown because of how dirty he was. We were ecstatic to have him back. Ariana decided to bathe him to wash off the dirt. After his not-welcomed bath, Rosie did not recognize him and kept hissing at him. After the whole ordeal was over, we began laughing at how poor Charlie went through hell and back only to return to where he had to be bathed and was no longer welcomed by Rosie.

My hope is that I can always find ways to look at things with less seriousness. It really helps turn our perspective around. If we take ourselves too seriously, we may end up being bitter and unable to later see the light. I choose happiness over depression! I hope everyone else does too.

REFLECTION QUESTIONS

1. What is an example of a time when you used humor to get through something difficult?
2. What are difficult situations that you have endured and can now look back and laugh at?
3. Is humor something that you practice; why or why not?
4. How do you feel when others use humor to make a tense situation lighter?

CHAPTER 9

INTELLIGENCE

Ironically, I could have chosen ignorance for the letter "I," but I opted for the positive word. However, I cannot avoid sharing about how seemingly intelligent people can also be ignorant in certain topics. What attracts me most to a person is intelligence, but I don't define intelligence the way many others do. I am not necessarily referring to people who have the highest IQs, the highest degrees, or who have the best employment positions. I am attracted to people who love learning, because to me that shows intelligence.

No matter the cognitive ability, the education level, or the position a person holds, there is always a need to keep learning. No one can ever know everything. When I present to groups of people, I always start by reminding them that I am no expert in anything except for one thing, which is my life. Even with thirty years of experience and having worked with thousands of students, I have never stopped learning.

I probably have average intelligence as measured by IQ, though when I was younger, I doubted even having average intelligence. Perhaps my doubts stemmed from always feeling that I had to prove myself and from experiences where I felt others questioned my intelligence because of my disability. Much later in life, I realized that I am very intelligent, not because I have superior scores in the traditional way of measuring intelligence but because I am persistent and have become a good learner. I am stubborn and when I make up my mind about something, I do my very best, no matter what it takes. Although I did not go through college with computers, Google, or various kinds of software, I feel that I am competent with computers. It doesn't come naturally, but I am able to teach myself about anything that I am interested in learning. I often refer to myself as a Millennial Wannabe because technology has opened so many doors for me, making me fearless in using it.

My daughters are much faster and often tease me by saying, "You love doing things the hard way." They show me how to do things in a matter of seconds compared to how long it takes me to do the same thing. My defense is always to say, "Remember, I am smarter than you. I got through college without computers, the Internet, YouTube, or Google." They just laugh and show me how to save lots of time doing things differently. However, once I learn it, I rarely forget how to do it again.

When I made the decision to venture into the publishing world, I knew that I had to start from square one. It was a new territory for me. However, step by step I was able to figure out how to do it, and then regretted not publishing earlier since I've always loved writing. However, I know that things happen at the time when they are supposed to happen. Now I've not only written and published two books, but I've also learned how to create my own website and to manage all my social media accounts to help me with marketing.

I am not book smart, but I am fine with that, because I have compensated for this with other skills that I excel in. When I say that I am not book smart, I mean that I am not one to remember statistics, authors, or facts. Everything I know is somehow relatable to me. I am not into filling my mind with details that are not applicable to me. I admire those researcher types but have accepted myself as I am. Our various skills, talents, and ways we show intelligence make this world interesting. This obligates us to work together as partners to complement each other and have better chances of succeeding in our objectives. I am the first one to admit that I need others to be successful.

I have met many people in my path who are very intelligent. Though my father never attended school, I considered him as having high intelligence. He taught himself how to read. He was very organized and knew where everything was placed. God forbid if we ever borrowed a tool and didn't return it where it belonged. He was very intelligent in the way he saw life. He was able to observe his surroundings and was always able to find a connection that taught us a lesson about life. I sometimes smile when I think about the fact that now there are manufacturing courses where students can learn to work with punch-press machinery, which he did for many years without an education. I can't help but wonder what he could have been if he'd had the opportunity to get an education. I don't know what he would have been, but I am certain that he would have succeeded.

My mother only went to school up to fifth grade, but I consider her one of the wisest women I have ever known. She had a tremendous problem-solving ability. She had to, to raise nine of us plus all our children as well. She was so skilled at gardening, likely having the skills of an educated botanist. She knew how to cross-pollinate flower plants, changing their color into beautiful combinations. If she'd had a formal education, I can't imagine all that she would have been able to do with her innate talent and love for plants.

Sometimes intelligence cannot be discovered because of the lack of equal opportunities for an education. I am certain that all my siblings are more naturally intelligent than I am. However, because they never sought an opportunity for higher education, they weren't always able to demonstrate how bright they are. Because of their work ethic and dedication, my siblings who worked found paths that led them to earn an income to support their families. As we kid around, we say, "There are no ignorant people in the Herrera family."

Both of my daughters are very intelligent. However, Ariel has a difficult time showing her intelligence due to her diagnosed learning disability and anxiety. This was true for many of the students I worked with at the college. It took me lots of effort to help Ariel and students like her to believe that their academic struggles were not based on intelligence. Most people believe that if there are academic difficulties, it is because of low intelligence or lack of effort. This is not always the case. In fact, to be diagnosed with learning disabilities, one of the criteria is to show that the IQ is average or above average. This regularly surprised students when I explained that the problem was due to a processing issue and not their intelligence. All their lives they thought they were dumb because of all their struggles.

Certainly, there are individuals with diagnosed intellectual disabilities. However, this doesn't mean that they cannot learn. Students who have intellectual disabilities, when they receive the appropriate education, can learn skills to make them employable. Such opportunities are available across the nation so that these students can be integrated into society. More programs like these need to be available and affordable.

As humans, we can't help but compare ourselves to others, always wanting to be smarter, have the highest degree, and have the highest position at work. However, I have learned that even those who have PhDs may be intelligent academically, but sometimes not personally. I have heard some insensitive comments from supposedly intelligent people who have advanced degrees. They lack any awareness of the inappropriateness of their words toward me as a person with a disability.

In my role at the college, I often attended professional conferences to keep up to date in the field of disability services. At one conference, during the opening keynote, my colleague Stacey and I sat at the table closest to the door. There were already several people sitting at the table. As I normally do, I introduced myself and greeted everyone. A woman sitting closest to me began talking to me. I noticed on her name tag that she was an administrator at a college and that she had a PhD. In small talk, she made a couple comments that Stacey and I, to this day, haven't forgotten. The woman said, "Oh, I saw another scooter. Maybe you can both have a race later." I had no idea how to respond. What was worse was that she continued making even more ignorant comments. After I explained my job at the college, saying that I helped students with disabilities to plan their accommodations and that I taught several classes, she said, "How do the students react to having you as their teacher when you are in a wheelchair?"

I couldn't believe that a highly educated woman wasn't aware of the inappropriateness of her commentary. Her first comment about racing was patronizing, making me feel like a child who needs to race, rather than the professional I am. Her second comment clearly demonstrated her lack of comfort with my being in a wheelchair. I wondered where she had been that she hadn't noticed that people with disabilities, when given the opportunity, can hold professional positions. Furthermore, our younger generations are now exposed to people with disabilities and many times are more accepting of differences, so my students never had any issues with my disability. I am sure some were surprised at first, but my disability disappeared once they were able to see that I could support them like anyone else or perhaps even better. This obviously intelligent woman showed her ignorance.

I am no longer impressed by levels of education. I am impressed with individuals who show their intelligence by being well-rounded and knowledgeable about others' experiences. We live in a multicultural world, so there is no excuse for being close minded about diversity. I am not saying that we should know everything about every marginalized group. What I am saying is that intelligent people should be aware of their lack of awareness and seek ways to learn more. Or, at the very least, follow one of the well-known golden rules: "If you don't have anything nice to say, then don't say anything at all."

In today's workforce, intelligence is not enough. We are required to be able to work with others. We are expected to get along with different employees. Students sometimes shared that they hated when their professors made them do group work. I reminded them that this was for their benefit. I shared that when people obtain jobs, they must be able to get along and work in partnership with their coworkers. Working in isolation is now very rare, so most workers must be prepared to work with others who may have different perspectives, opinions, and work styles.

I was part of many interview committees when there were faculty or administrator position searches at the college. Meeting the minimum educational requirements was all we cared about in terms of levels of education. What really mattered was how the applicant responded to our prepared questions, which often related to working in groups, their leadership style, and questions about their knowledge of diversity. Sure, the qualifications were important, but what mattered most was demonstrating a different type of intelligence. For lack of a better word, individuals need to demonstrate "life" intelligence.

Again, it took me my entire career to realize that level of education is not the only measure of intelligence. Of course, I am not dismissing the great accomplishments of those who obtain a PhD, but I have stopped comparing my education to those of others as a way to gauge my level of intelligence. Just like I don't consider myself smarter than members of my family who did not go to college, I shouldn't think of myself as less intelligent because I only have a master's degree.

I used to think that each of us was born with a certain level of intelligence. In fact, when I was obtaining my master's in education with a reading and learning disability concentration, we focused a lot on learning the different categories of levels of IQ. They drilled into our brains the different breakdowns. For example, we learned that average intelligence had to fall between 80 and 110 IQ points, and that, to label a person with learning disabilities, they had to at least have an IQ of 80.

However, through the years, I noticed those numbers were being manipulated so that, in their minds, students could receive the more acceptable label. I had students whose IQ fell below 80 but who still came in with documentation that labeled them as having learning disabilities. For some reason, families felt that the LD label was more acceptable than the intellectual disability label. However, students and parents soon found out that college expectations were higher than what the student was able to achieve. Sometimes the achievement gaps were so big that this often ended up being frustrating for the student and the faculty member alike.

Unfortunately, I do not have the answers. As an educator, I was interested in helping each student succeed regardless of the label they received. Students deserve an opportunity, but the opportunity should be where the student can thrive and learn and not just get frustrated. It's like gardening.

If a plant is withering because of too much sun, then we move it to the shade. We all have challenges we need to accept. Just like I can never be a flight attendant because of my inability to walk, some students may not be able to complete a college credential. However, this doesn't mean that the student can't succeed. Why do we always want to measure success based on the traditional measures of GPA and completion of a credential? Some students' intention might be to just experience college life or to improve on a skill. To them, the ability to do that might equal success.

Levels of intelligence should not be yet another reason to divide people. No one is better than the next person. We were all created with the same love and devotion and are in this world to serve a mission. Treating everyone with respect, regardless of intellect measures, is all that should matter. If we are to live in this complex world, the sooner we accept ourselves and others regardless of our measured levels of intelligence, the sooner we will live in harmony.

REFLECTION QUESTIONS

1. In what ways do you consider yourself intelligent?
2. When in your life have you lacked intelligence?
3. To you, how do others in your life show intelligence?
4. Has anyone ever made you feel that you were not intelligent? If yes, how?

CHAPTER 10

JUSTICE

Perhaps because I have had a disability for as long as I can remember, I have always been an advocate of justice. However, my definition of justice changed over time because of my professional development and my personal life. In the past, I used to think that advocating for justice meant fighting so that everyone was treated the same way or equally. However, as I grew professionally and personally, I learned that being just is not necessarily treating everyone the same, but rather that each person is entitled to receive what they need.

When I started working at Harper, the ADA had just been signed into law. I saw my role as being an advocate for students so that they were treated fairly and equally. I quickly noticed that this definition of advocacy was contradictory when I was approving accommodations based on the functional limitations of my students, and I was requesting that faculty treat the students with disabilities differently by facilitating their approved accommodation. Students with disabilities needed accommodations such as extended time on tests and the use of note takers so they would have access helping them to succeed. Understandably, some of the professors felt that it would not be fair for some students to get more time on a test when other students didn't. They questioned whether this different treatment would be unfair. Most of the time, they accepted my explanation of why the different treatment was just. I would explain that the students who are approved for accommodations are disadvantaged from the get-go compared to their classmates without disabilities and that the accommodations were simply to even the playing field, not to give them an unfair advantage.

Some people struggle with understanding that justice doesn't mean that everyone gets the same treatment, at the same time, in the same way. I admit that I often wished people would see me as a person and not see my disability. I didn't want special treatment because of my disability because I thought it would be unfair. What I should have been saying is that people should see me as a person with a disability who may require accommodations because of my physical limitations. Being disabled is part of my identity, just like being a Latina woman is also part of my identity. The intersectionality of my identities makes me a whole person. If one of those identities is overlooked or ignored, then part of who I am is being ignored. For there to be justice, each part of each person needs to be considered.

My parents modeled this without me even realizing it. I have eight brothers and sisters, and we are all different. We have different skills, different personalities, different abilities, and different goals. My parents knew that about all of us and for this reason they treated us all differently. I'm sure at times that some of us may have seen their treatment as unfair, but ultimately, what they were really doing was being just.

We were raised in a traditional Mexican family. My parents instilled values that represented our culture. The females in the house had responsibilities that the males didn't, and vice versa. I am sure that my older sisters sometimes may have viewed this as unfair because my parents were stricter with them than my brothers. But my brothers probably felt the same for different reasons. As a female with a disability, my parents treated me even more differently. This did not mean that they didn't have expectations of me. They were just very aware of each of our capabilities, and the responsibilities given at home revolved around those differences. Unfortunately, being treated differently did not save me from having to wash dishes just because I was in a wheelchair! My parents always considered the adjustments that were needed for me to meet the obligation of washing dishes. Although I did not have access to our laundry room because of its size, my parents still expected me to do my laundry, just with some help. Maybe that is why I hate folding clothes! I consider loading the washer and transferring the clothes to the dryer the fun and easy part, but those are the tasks I needed assistance with when doing my laundry. I was left with the not-so-fun part—folding clothes.

I lived an independent life at home. My dad was always willing to make modifications so that I could be as independent as possible. When the closet was too high for me to hang up my clothes, my father figured out a way to lower the clothing rod so that I could reach it. Similarly, because I enjoyed cooking at times, my mother made sure to keep the ingredients I used on a regular basis in the lowest cabinet. If I needed something from up high, she would get it down for me. Depending on what it was, sometimes I would just use a Reacher, which I had practically in every room. (A Reacher, which is sometimes referred to as a Grabber, is a reach extender with a handle that allows people to reach high items by operating a clawlike mechanism to clasp them with.) I didn't know it then, but basically, they were accommodating me because of my disability.

My oldest brother had more expectations as the oldest male. Mom and dad ensured that he would walk a straight line by going to school and working. I believe that my mother was more present with him because of her worry that my brother might make the wrong decisions and get involved with friends who would lead him into trouble. As a result, my brother is a hard-working man who plays the role of a patriarch now that my dad is no longer with us.

As the youngest daughter, my parents were more lenient with me. I am not sure if my parents were more lenient with me than my sisters because they knew that my life was different or because they got tired of being so strict after parenting my five older sisters. Still, I wonder why they allowed me to travel, stay out at night, and do pretty much anything school-related when my sisters had to beg to even be able to go to the movies. Was this just? I think it was. We all just trusted that my parents always knew why they made the decisions they did.

Women in my family play an important role in a household, and high morals and decency are expected. I believe my parents had to guard my sisters so that they would not end up in bad relationships or end up getting pregnant before marriage. This was a huge reason why I ended up believing that I would never marry and that I'd live with my parents my entire life. I thought, if my parents don't expect me to have the same responsibilities as my sisters and I don't have to abide by the same rules, it must be because they think I will never get married or become pregnant. Although I never asked my parents why I was treated differently, I trust that they knew what they were doing. All my sisters married by the age of twenty-one, and all of them are still married. In fact, my oldest sister, Bella, celebrated her 50th wedding anniversary in August 2022. My mom's living room looked like a photography studio because of all our wedding pictures on the walls. So, my parents' ways may have appeared unjust because we were all treated differently, but their approach worked, as evidenced by us all finding long-lasting, loving relationships.

If I were to ask each brother and sister if they thought they were loved by my parents, each one would say yes, and furthermore, each would say that they were the person my mom loved most. I know I feel that way. What this means is that even if we ever felt that the treatment we received was unjust, it never affected our perceptions of how much we were loved. I don't know how they did it, but they were incredible parents.

Now that I am a parent myself, having two girls with only seven months difference in age, I am beginning to understand justice at home more clearly. Ariel and Ariana are completely different in personality, temperament, and behavior. Ariel is likely to say that I was stricter with her as an adolescent and that I scolded her most. She would be right. Sometimes, I would reflect and question myself about whether I was being fair or not in the way I disciplined my daughters. I always concluded that the reason I treated Ariel with more discipline was because she needed it. Ariana was compliant, didn't push my buttons, and did what she had to do in school and at home. Why would I discipline her like Ariel when Ariana mostly obeyed the rules and completed her responsibilities? There was hardly any reason to scold or discipline.

My hope is that when they are older and look back on their childhoods, they will both say that I loved them equally although I might not have treated them the same. Love was present even when I was strict, got angry, got frustrated, and most of all when I was disciplining them. When I showed tough love, I was likely hurting more than they were. I love them both equally, but I know each one needs different ways for me to show it. I always reminded the girls that discipline is the most important way to show love, something I learned from Father John. Hopefully they believed me.

I have always had a vested interest in fighting for justice by participating in groups focusing on diversity, equity, and inclusion. The names of such groups have changed over the years, but the mission and goals have remained the same. When I first started working in the 1990s, believe it or not, the committee that focused on diversity was called "Affirmative Action." I collaborated with colleagues on these committees to ensure that students, regardless of their identities, received just treatment. I'm happy to see that the word "equity" is now used regularly, because it's a better term for describing justice for everyone. In my opinion, "belonging" would be even better because that would mean that justice is in practice.

In life, some people may believe that God is not just because of their life circumstances or problems. Sometimes it is hard to understand justice when we hear about young children being killed because of gun violence. We often say, "Life isn't fair." And if we analyze people's lives closely, sometimes we can't help but to agree with this. Why are there starving children? Why do people get serious diseases? Why was I the only one in my family to get polio? Why do some people get the opportunity for an education whereas others do not? Why do parents have to bury their children because of an accident or a disease? Why is wealth so unevenly divided? So many questions without answers.

Sometimes I think my own life is unjust, but that is because I lose sight of my blessings. I complain and say that it is so unfair that everything is much more difficult for me. Yet again, I don't mention that I have so many privileges, most of the time unearned, over so many others. In God's perfection, I am sure He is just. We may not see it, but I pray that it becomes crystal clear after we leave this earth.

It is easy to blame God for allowing all these injustices to happen. But where is our responsibility? Shouldn't we help to bring justice? Each one of us can do something to better our lives and the world we live in. We are so quick to be greedy instead of sharing with others, so quick to be judgmental instead of accepting others' differences, so quick to be violent instead of being peaceful, too quick to be selfish and worry only about ourselves instead of being helpful to others, and so quick to be hostile instead of friendly. The choice is always ours, and, at least in our immediate circles, we can make a difference.

In a just world there would be peace and harmony. But it is hard work. It requires love for others when many times we do not even love ourselves. It requires giving rather than receiving. It requires being open to differences and accepting people for who they are instead of being racist, homophobic, ableist, sexist, and otherwise discriminatory. I know I may be dreaming and writing about a world that doesn't exist. But I can only hope that we each try to do our part so that justice can be a reality. If we need something to motivate us to be just, we must remember that it is only when we are just that we receive justice.

REFLECTION QUESTIONS

1. How do you show justice in your life?
2. How have you been treated unjustly?
3. How can you practice justice regularly in your life?
4. What is an example of when you were accused of being unjust?
5. What steps can you take to advocate for justice in our world?

CHAPTER 11

KARMA

WHEN I THINK OF KARMA, TWO PHRASES I LEARNED IN THE PAST COME to mind. The first phrase I remember vividly from when I was learning English; I was interested in learning a variety of sayings to improve my vocabulary and to inspire me. The quote that I am reminded of is from Confucius, and it says, "Don't do unto others what you don't want done unto you." I believe that the phrase is commonly used to teach children to be kind and respectful, which is a very important lesson to learn. Karma also reminds me of a second phrase, which was used as part of the Hippocratic oath for medical professionals. This one says, "I will abstain from all intentional wrongdoing and harm." To me, both phrases mean being passive but also not participating in doing wrong. Although it is a good start, Karma takes us a step further. Not only should we not do harm, but also, if we do, it will come back to us. The way I picture it is that what we do is like a boomerang that always comes back. This gives us the power to determine what happens in our lives.

To be honest, I am not sure if I believe in Karma. First, it takes away God's power. I often observe how bad things happen to good people and good things happen to bad people. If Karma existed, it would make better sense if bad things happened to bad people and good things happened to good people. As always, I have more questions than answers. I know that some people use the fear of Karma as a motivator to deter them from doing or wishing someone harm.

Regardless of whether Karma exists or not, what I am certain of is that, most of the time, we are compensated for our good actions and deeds. Case in point, I worked very hard at the college and genuinely sought to help each student I worked with every semester. I was rewarded tenfold for my dedication not only in recognition I received from the college, but most importantly, in the appreciation I received from students and their families. I have always found that the kindness I give by caring for people and always trying to help them is always returned to me.

Similarly, I am always amazed at how I am rewarded when I am generous. There have been times when we make monetary donations and then get a check in the mail unexpectedly. It's as if our good deed was being compensated. Other times, I have been surprised by gestures of kindness because of something I did. Most of the time, I didn't think it was a big deal and saw it as part of my job, but students found meaningful ways to show their appreciation.

I am not sure if those are examples of Karma, because I have always believed that God is in control. I remember my dad telling me, "No se mueve la hoja del árbol sin la voluntad de Dios," which means "a tree leaf does not move without God's will." This saying was a reminder that God is in control of everything. With a belief in Karma, we are the cause of what happens to us and not God.

Although I believe God is in control, I do think that being kind and doing good deeds is satisfying. I know that when I focus on myself, it often leads to sadness. In a way, I volunteer and try to help others because I gain more than I give. There is such satisfaction when I see the success of students I helped. In a way, I hope that I had a tiny bit to do with their success. I am a firm believer that we should use any thing or any belief that ultimately helps us do what is good and right. Helping others is part of our responsibility.

Just recently, I gave a presentation at a nursing home facility where I ran into a student I worked with in the past. Scott was a young man who had been classified as behaviorally disordered because of his inability to control his anger. We worked together for two years; he chose to see me once a week for the entire time he was a student. He referred to these appointments as his accountability check-ins. What we did most was to talk about strategies to combat his anger, coming up with better approaches so that he could have better impulse control. We talked about situations in his life, and I helped him see things from a different perspective so that he could consider them without anger. At the nursing home, I had the opportunity to chat with some residents and with Scott for a few minutes. I was so pleased to hear that he has been working at the nursing home and that the residents love him. Seeing his success is so gratifying. My hard work with him helped him to be a better person and helped him to be happier.

As I go around to libraries, book clubs, schools, and book fairs to talk about my life and share my book *Not Always a Valley of Tears*, I am always humbled by the comments I receive from my audiences. It is satisfying to hear that all the hard work I did and sacrifices I made to overcome my many obstacles are helping others. Because of what I share during my presentations, I have met several people who are motivated to seek my support because of their interest in self-publishing.

I met the kindest Columbian woman, who is now a dear friend. She shared that she had been writing poetry for years but never figured out how to even begin to think about publishing. She is so motivated now and continues to write with hopes of publishing her collection soon. Additionally, I went to do a presentation about my book to the Bilingual Parent Advisory Council (BPAC) from Mannheim School District 83, a group in my community. The parents in the group were so motivated that they asked me to do writing workshops so that they could write short vignettes and publish a collection of their individual stories. How amazing is that? Also, just this week, a woman who lives far from me read my book and asked if she could visit me because she too aspires to be an author. I may not be making mega money from publishing my book, but I am being compensated in more meaningful ways by helping others to pursue their own dreams.

These are all examples of the good that is resulting from my hard work and sharing my story. As I help others, I am rewarded in ways I never would have imagined. Throughout my life, I find that any good I do for my community is always well recognized and that I gain as much or more than I give. I believe this is likely to be true for anyone who helps others. It's no mistake that many of my friends who have retired are now volunteers for their respective passions. Obviously, our work is not because of money but because of the satisfaction of knowing that we are making a difference.

All I can say is that our life's joy is measured by the joy we give others. It's a simple rule whether we believe in Karma or not. When we are generous, our generosity is returned. When we are kind, our kindness is returned. When we smile, a smile is returned. However, when we are selfish, isolation and loneliness are assured. When we are mean, anger is returned. When we frown, a frown is returned. Isn't it better to have the better things returned?

Being part of a big family has been my greatest treasure. When my mother was still alive, she was the connection between us all. She taught us to always be kind to one another. It is foreign for me to hear about broken families and examples of siblings who don't get along or stop speaking to each other. My mom ensured that we wouldn't talk negatively about each other. If any of us started complaining about something a sibling did, she would nip it at the bud and immediately fix the discord. She knew that whatever we gave, the same would be returned. Instead of wanting us to be mad at each other, she taught us to accept each other as we were. She taught us to love each other no matter what.

Now that she is gone, we continue the great life lessons she gave us. We are always there to support each other. We do not hold grudges and accept that each person has his or her own point of view. The family bond is always something I have valued. No matter what happens in my life, I know there will be eight brothers and sisters and their families ready to support me. Likewise, when any of them is in need, I am present. We celebrate each of our birthdays with well wishes, small gifts, and, above all, love. I guess we reap what we sow. Karma?

Some people believe in Karma or have other beliefs, ranging from believing in spells to witchcraft, to explain what happens in life. I was raised not to believe in anything other than what the Catholic church teaches. I know people who believe that their child is ill because of getting "mal de ojo" or the "evil eye." Again, I believe this is because of their desire to explain something that is going wrong. In some cultures, there is a genuine belief that harm can be caused just by a bad wish or a bad look. I am skeptical about these beliefs, though I understand how people may want to find a cause to explain their suffering.

My parents always pushed us away from practicing any of those beliefs. Similarly, I have taught my girls that there is always a scientific reason for an illness and when there isn't, God is the only explanation. I am firm in this belief. When I was an infant of nine months, I was always in the care of a family member. I wasn't yet walking, so there is no way I could have been exposed to anything that another member in my family hadn't been. I got the polio virus and no one else in my family did. I have never found a logical, scientific explanation of why I was the only one who contracted polio. Was it a spell cast upon me? Did I get "mal de ojo?" Was it Karma returning to me and my family because of something bad we did? Was there witchcraft involved that caused my paralysis? I say no to all these questions. God's will is the only explanation I have ever found.

Then there is the question, if God is so loving, why was it His will that I get polio? Again, there could be a multitude of reasons. However, toward the end of my mother's life, I found a satisfying answer for me. I had to be disabled. Period. Because it is through this disability that I have been able to help so many people. I see myself as God's instrument. In fact, I have jokingly said that God should be listed as my coauthor for every book I write. My faith is rooted in the belief that God doesn't want suffering or pain.

I am not suffering more than the next person. My disability has not made my life unbearable. On the contrary, sometimes I believe that my disability has made my life better. I don't see it as a curse or something bad. I am certain that everyone hurts and suffers, even when they have perfectly functioning legs. I hope that God continues to use me as an instrument to speak loudly and make people understand that my life is not miserable because of my disability.

Of course, life's barriers do affect me. These barriers need to be fixed, not my inability to walk. My legs are perfectly fine and don't need fixing, contrary to what most people think. I don't get up each morning wishing that I'd no longer be disabled, that I would suddenly be able to walk. I just pray for patience and understanding for the people who say or do things that are hurtful. I pray for this world to be as God intended it. I will strive to do my part to make it happen.

Karma, or any other belief, should lead people to do their best to live harmoniously with others. It's important to know that good should win over evil. We must know that no matter what our life situation is, we are strong enough to handle it. Nothing will be unbearable. We must look at our lives and reflect on how we can help others, which will result in us being our own very best selves.

REFLECTION QUESTIONS

1. Do you believe in karma? If so, how does it affect your life?
2. What unique beliefs or practices exist in your family?
3. How do you think that good deeds are rewarded in life? Bad deeds?

CHAPTER 12
LOYALTY

LOYALTY IS A CHARACTERISTIC THAT WE ALWAYS LOOK FOR IN ANY RELA-tionship we have. But loyalty is much more than faithfulness in relation-ships. When someone is not loyal, trust is broken, making it difficult to sustain the relationship. This characteristic is necessary in friendships and families, among husbands and wives, but especially with ourselves. Because I want people in my life to be loyal, I try to practice loyalty in every aspect of my life.

There are many types of tools to determine personality types and strengths. At Harper, I had the opportunity to take Gallup's StrengthsFinder assessment. The test is meant to indicate people's top five strengths based on how questions are answered. My results showed that one of my top five strengths is that I am an includer. I wasn't surprised that includer was one of my strengths. I'd like to believe that this is because I strive to be loyal, and one way that I demonstrate that is by including everyone, regardless of the status of the person. To me, we are all equal, whether a person is a gardener, unemployed, a teacher, an attorney, a doctor, a millionaire, homeless, or any other type of status in life. This viewpoint has been ben-eficial for me since I have been able to develop many partnerships with a diverse group of people, always making my life interesting and better.

In the Access and Disability Services (ADS) department at Harper College, I had the honor of working with a team that I saw as family. There were eight of us, some part-time and some full-time. We worked hard, trusted each other, had fun, and collaborated on developing programs that supported students with disabilities. And, we must not forget, we also ate a lot—often in celebration, but also just because. Food always made our jobs easier. What matters most, though, is that we were all committed to our work. We were loyal to our students and did whatever we could to support them.

I know this type of work group environment is ideal but difficult to find, so I consider myself very fortunate to have had my Harper family. As a full-time faculty and Coordinator of Learning Services, I was responsible for supervising and completing the evaluations of non-faculty staff positions and the part-time learning specialist positions. Having this type of responsibility did not change our group's dynamic, because I considered everyone equally as part of the team regardless of our titles or responsibilities. I worked hard in maintaining a trusting work environment. This required being transparent, honest, and a good communicator. I saw the program as *our* program, and not *my* program.

Although we had the good fortune to work together for many years, for multiple reasons out of our control, the group dwindled toward the end of my career. Even though we all took different paths, I continue to be friends with them, and I will always be loyal to each one of them. I am confident that they will be loyal to me as well. Loyalty connected us and made us better at our jobs. Together we were better than each of us individually.

Friendships outside of my department were also developed because of loyalty. I was always honest and genuine in my desire to support faculty, especially when working with mutually challenging students. Because of my role, I worked with many faculty, from all disciplines, who later became friends. They knew they could count on me. Faculty were fully aware that I would do anything to help the students be successful, which resulted in me helping them to be successful as teachers also. Besides working with faculty, I also worked with many staff on programming for Harper students.

It was evident that because of my loyalty, I developed strong bonds with many staff members from all areas of the college. Even after retirement, those connections have not ended.

First and foremost, I was loyal to my students and their families. I advocated for their needs because I never doubted their ability to succeed. I always saw the potential in my students even when they had a poor academic record or severe disabilities. Sometimes, I believed in them more than they believed in themselves. Students trusted me and were comfortable talking to me about anything. They realized that I understood them because I was speaking from my heart. They knew we shared the same lived experience as individuals with disabilities. Even during some difficult conversations with students where I had to address their failing grades or their inappropriate behavior, students knew that I cared and wanted their success. Some of the difficult conversations resulted in the greatest growth for the student and for me.

Loyalty requires a commitment to be there for the other. The commitment is natural and not forced because both really care for one another. Mutual loyalty is a requirement in any healthy relationship. One person cannot be loyal while the other person is unfaithful. Once loyalty is broken, it will be difficult to repair and rebuild the trust. This often ends up ruining the bond of the two individuals, whether it is friendship, marriage, or any other type of partnership. In these cases, the most difficult decision to be made is if the betrayed individual should stay in the relationship or whether it is best to walk away from it. Sometimes a person must walk away not because they're giving up, but because they realize that they deserve better.

Loyalty was always an expectation in my family. My parents were married for fifty-eight years when my dad passed away. If they were still alive now, I am certain they would still be united. Likewise, none of my siblings or I have ever divorced. If my mom ever heard us complaining about our spouses, she quickly interceded saying that we had to be loyal and work things out with the goal of reconciliation and staying married. The word *divorce* never entered our vocabulary. Marriage is difficult, and I am sure my siblings and I have sometimes felt like giving up because of problems with our spouses. However, because there hasn't been any abuse of any kind, resolutions have been possible. Unfortunately, that is not always the case in some marriages. Sometimes walking away is the only option left.

My parents modeled loyalty in how they lived their marriage and lives. My mom lived for my dad and for us. She was dedicated entirely to the family, with gardening being her only diversion. My friends couldn't believe it when I would tell them that my mom never spent time with friends, attended concerts, went to the movies, or vacationed. Our family was her entire life. Likewise, my dad was not only loyal to my mom and his children, but also constantly voiced how my mother was the love of his life and how much we all meant to him. He would say, "I am nothing without your mom and my family." I never feared that my parents would someday break apart, not even when my dad was dealing with his alcoholism. They were committed to each other and always found a way to resolve their differences.

I previously mentioned how my parents showed each of their children how to be there for one another. Even today, I can trust my brothers and sisters with my struggles, and they would be ready to give me support and/or advice. I have good relationships with all of them. They know that I adore my family and that I thank God every day for blessing me with all of them as my siblings. Having a disability all my life has been bearable because of the family I was born into. Sure, at times we have disagreements or even a spat here and there, but I am honest when I say that I have never held a grudge or resentment toward any of my brothers or sisters. And I believe they haven't either.

I hope that Isidro and I are also modeling loyalty to both our daughters. First, in our relationship with each other, then in our relationships with both of them. I also expect that the girls will be loyal to each other. I have taught them to be honest and to help each other, especially if one of them is making a bad decision. When they were teens, I walked a thin line between telling them not to tattle so that they could be loyal to each other and telling them to inform me if one of them was in danger. They looked out for each other, and I loved how they were straightforward and transparent. They never talked behind each other's backs. They made sure that if they told me about one another, that the sister be present too.

Nowadays, it is uncommon to have long-lasting marriages. More and more couples are ending up in divorce for many reasons, including infidelity. I know that commitments require a lot of work and effort. Some couples may find that there is no solution for infidelity or other demonstrations of betrayals, since trust is broken. When couples get married, typically they intend to live happily ever after. I realize that sometimes there are legitimate reasons for having to divorce, but hopefully before divorcing the couple has made attempts to resolve their conflicts.

Loyalty within any relationship serves as a bond that brings peace. We all need to have the support of loved ones, and we depend on the loyalty of others to help us when we are in need. Each person has the responsibility to show that they are trustworthy. Peace is greatly disturbed when a relationship is full of conflict, abuse, or lack of respect. To live in a safe and happy relationship, both parties must be equally invested in making things work. It might involve compromise and sometimes forgiveness. Above all, it requires communication and an honest decision to make things work regardless of what it takes. Sometimes it may mean staying when desiring to leave.

Conflict between people will always exist. But one of the best ways to avoid conflict is to make the commitment to remain loyal. For the sake of the marriage and family, each partner must work to avoid temptations that may lead to infidelity. Infidelity and betrayal are the most hurtful ways to show lack of loyalty. It won't only destroy a loved one's peace, but may also destroy that person's own peace of mind.

Besides being loyal to those around me, it has always been important to be loyal to myself—the full self. I must accept each part of my identities, live authentically as I am, and be loyal to my values, even when I may be misunderstood or judged. I find it imperative not to hide who I am. Likewise, I have always attempted to teach my daughters to do the same.

When Ariana was in second grade, one of her assignments was to create a poster that had the heading "Hot Banana" with questions underneath that she had to answer. The list included questions such as *What is your favorite color, what is your favorite Disney movie, what is your favorite food,* etc. We worked on the assignment together. When we got to the question about her favorite food, she quickly responded, "tacos de lengua" or beef tongue tacos. My mom, who was her caregiver while I worked, often cooked beef tongue, chopping it up to use as the meat for tacos.

The next day, when Ariana came home from school, she was not happy with the reaction she got from her classmates when she shared her "Hot Banana" poster. She said that her classmates were grossed out when she said she loved tongue tacos. With conviction, she exclaimed, "From now on, I am going to say spaghetti is my favorite food." Even from this early age, she was forming the opinion that being her true self was not going to be appreciated or understood. Although I tried to convince her that there was nothing funny, gross, or wrong about liking tongue tacos, I understood why she preferred to conform with what others would accept instead of being honest.

I understood Ariana's dilemma because, even as an adult, I sometimes did the same thing. Sometimes I felt that I had to stop being Mexican as soon as I got to work. While traveling to work, I listened to my Spanish music, singing along to the songs. As soon as I got inside the building where my department was housed, though, I felt a change in me. It's as if I switched hats and no longer could be Mexican. My behavior was different, I thought differently, and I even liked different things. If I had been asked what kind of music I liked, I would have never mentioned Los Bukis, the music I listened to when I drove in to work. Instead, I would have said that I loved Bon Jovi.

Even my behavior and how I saw my disability changed depending on if I was at work or at home. At work, I always wanted to prove my independence, so even if I was struggling, I'd wait until someone would offer to help, and even then, I'd often be hesitant to accept it. For instance, whenever there was a social event at work where food was served in a buffet style, I'd carefully decide where to sit so that I could independently grab my food. If food items were too high and I couldn't reach them, I'd just choose something else to eat that was more accessible. If I really, really wanted something, like chocolate-covered strawberries, I would ask a close friend to help.

Yet at home, whenever there is a family gathering, I often find a corner to sit in and stay there until I go home. Without fail, several family members will bring me a plate with a variety of the food being served. On some occasions, I even had to give the plates back because someone else had already brought me food. With family, I felt obligated to accept my role of being cared for and dependent. I guess I felt that that was the expectation, so I just conformed to it.

I am not sure which behavior, how I acted at home or how I acted at work, represents the real me and which behavior I changed to meet others' expectations. Am I as dependent as I am with my family? Or am I just pretending to be dependent, allowing myself to be served to satisfy the expectations that my family members had of me? At work, was the real me the independent woman I showed up as? Or was I acting the part to model how I hoped people would see individuals with disabilities? At my age, I still wonder who I really am. Are both behaviors me? Am I being loyal to myself in both instances? Do I change my behavior based on the environment? Though cultural frame switching is common with diverse individuals in terms of race and culture, I've experienced it with disability instead.

Even with this conflict, I have always been loyal to my values everywhere I go. However, in one experience, I had to be unknowingly pushed to be loyal to my values. During the first social justice demonstration I took part in, I wasn't sure how to live my values. I believed in fighting for the rights of people with disabilities but wasn't in agreement with the possibility of getting arrested, which I heard might happen when participating in civil disobedience demonstrations. I had made the decision to avoid getting arrested, thinking that it would not be favorable for a college professor to get a citation for breaking the law, even when it was a misdemeanor. However, in the excitement of the protest, and by seeing how so many individuals with more serious disabilities fought without concern for themselves or arrests, I immediately realized that if I was loyal to the cause, I should stop being concerned for my own personal well-being. I believe that when we believe in something with all our being, concern about personal consequences should disappear.

Being loyal to our values and principles is so fulfilling. It wasn't until I focused on my desire to bring about positive change for individuals with disabilities that I was living my true values. This experience made me bolder, and it helped me to understand that speaking out against injustice, even when it is not a popular thing to do, is respecting myself and my values. From then on, I have always posed this question to myself: "Is this cause important enough for me to get arrested?"

We live in a country where we have the freedom to speak freely about our beliefs and have the freedom to advocate for the changes that matter most to us. If we are loyal to ourselves and conduct peaceful demonstrations without violence, we will feel that we are doing something for what we believe. Sometimes that is not possible, though, and when it isn't, we must be prepared for resistance. Any fight for positive change will likely be addressed with resistance, but this is the only way to make a difference so that we can all live with equity.

As an author, I am being loyal to myself with each sentence I write. I do not know if readers will react negatively to what I write. I hope not. However, most authors make themselves vulnerable in sharing their stories, ideas, knowledge, and opinions that matter to them. Sure, I could try to please all readers, but I am fully aware that that will never be possible. I am so loyal to my viewpoints that I am willing to expose them regardless of the readership's reactions. The experiences I share with short stories have taught me a lot about life, and I hope that by sharing them, it will be useful for people to reflect on their own lives. As I mentioned in my introduction, I am smarter than to think that everyone will agree with my opinions. I don't expect, nor do I want, readers to instantly change their thoughts, viewpoints, or opinions just from reading what I've written. In fact, that would be missing the point about what I am sharing. I want each person to be loyal to their own beliefs. But what I do hope is that readers will analyze their thoughts and, through that process, gain something that can make life more joyful for them.

Being loyal to ourselves does not mean that we must be stubborn and not be open to changing our viewpoints. I constantly change my own viewpoints, but I do so without ignoring my values. My own daughters have helped me change viewpoints. Because I had a good example of how I was raised by my parents, I wanted to raise my girls as my parents did. However, times are different, so I've had to be flexible. I cannot impose my stubbornness without looking at what is going on around me. My girls, as little as they were, showed me that giving them room to make mistakes was good parenting. For example, for a long time, I resisted allowing them to use technology, fearing the danger of being connected with strangers. However, I soon realized that by resisting, I was disadvantaging them because other children their age were freely using the internet. Instead, I allowed them to use technology and helped them make decisions about what was safe and what was not. I was still being true to the values I learned from my parents.

Loyalty to the self is the first step. Being true to ourselves makes us credible, and people will want to listen. I loved when people at work would share that they knew where I stood (so to speak!) no matter what was on the table for discussion. I didn't even have to open my mouth. My reputation was that I was passionately student-centered. On occasion, I was complimented for speaking for students whose voices were often ignored. My message was always the same regardless of where I was on campus or what project I worked on. My song and dance, as I often referred to it, was that students with disabilities and Latino students can be successful given the opportunities and support they need. I never compromised this message, even when I knew it might be opposed because of cost, difficulty, or lack of understanding.

Living our authentic selves and being loyal to our beliefs is a choice we all have. Of course, sometimes it will be a difficult choice, but nonetheless, when we choose to be real, we will be appreciated by the people who really matter—our families and friends. But we have to be loyal to ourselves before we can be loyal to anyone else.

REFLECTION QUESTIONS

1. What. or who are you most loyal to in your life?
2. When has loyalty been challenging for you?
3. How do you show loyalty to yourself?
4. What changes do you need to make to be more loyal?

CHAPTER 13
MOTIVATION

I USED TO TELL STUDENTS THAT GAS IS TO A CAR AS MOTIVATION IS TO LIFE. Both would be stuck and unable to move forward without them. Of course, we cannot just drive up to a gas station to fill up with motivation. We must figure out how to find our own motivation. Sometimes the motivation can be external, such as wanting to get an education to get better opportunities for a job. Or perhaps motivation to exercise three times a week to lose weight to be able wear the wedding dress that fits perfectly. External motivation usually offers a reward at the end.

Motivation can also come from internally without the need to be rewarded. I have found that with internal motivation, I have received more fulfillment, which usually leads me to greater rewards than I ever expected. What we sometimes forget is that, with fulfillment, we are more prone to be passionate about doing well in our jobs, at school, and in other parts of our life. As a result, this motivation is often recognized by awards, scholarships, or better pay. I am sure each person can find their own source of internal motivation. For me, it goes back to almost dying when I was first diagnosed with polio.

Because of the many stories I heard from my parents, siblings, and other family members, I have always seen my life as a miracle. This has been the engine driving everything I do, stopping me from ever giving up, regardless of the struggles in front of me. My internal motivation is rooted in the thought that God allowed me to wake up from my paralysis because he had a purpose for me. I am here for a reason, just like everyone else is. My motivation stems from wanting to earn the privilege of living. I work hard, get through struggles, and endure suffering so that I can thank God for not taking me when I contracted polio. I have always looked for the next job, the next goal, the next accomplishment, but most of all, the next opportunity to help others in living a better life. By being honest and open about my life, I think it inspires others to believe in their dreams. I feel that I am expected to do the very best in my life.

For this reason, I have always had a difficult time saying no to requests. But as I age, I realize that I cannot do everything and do it well. I am getting more comfortable with prioritization and am gentler with myself when I say no. I realize that I cannot do everything, so I try to focus on things that will be fulfilling to me while having the greatest impact on others. The expectations I put on myself are high. I do not know how to sit on the sidelines. Perhaps this is because I have so often been excluded from participation because of physical barriers, so I have learned to hate being just a spectator. If I can do something, I will do it!

If I were asked why I think I am expected to say yes to every request, I'd answer that it is because I have that expectation of myself. Some of these behaviors come from my upbringing and other parts may be genetic. My mother modeled how we should always act immediately today and not wait for mañana, reminding us that tomorrow may never come. This worked in my favor most of the time, though I am sure that I could have prevented a lot of unnecessary stress if I didn't always put this pressure on myself. At school, at work, and at home, I met my responsibilities without any pro-crastination. Sometimes, I push myself to the limit to get everything done.

Though I am aging, my motivation is stronger than ever, but there is a shadow side to everything. Because of my extreme motivation, I set seemingly unmanageable goals for myself. And, surprisingly, I usually meet these unrealistic goals and, most of the time, I am even ahead of schedule. But I must analyze and ask myself, "At what cost?" Others have commented that what I get done is impressive. As I reflect, I wonder why I feel that I need to keep proving myself. I just keep going, rarely taking time to just rest. I don't watch much TV, and it is dreadful for me when my family wants to go to the movies. Going to the movies means having to sit still for two hours without being able to multitask. To me that is difficult.

My daughter recently asked me why I work so much now that I am retired. She even questioned if I was doing it for financial reasons, which often is a great motivator for many people. I didn't have to think about it long. I told her that I didn't retire; I just rewired, something Father John pointed out to me. Besides, when I work, I forget my disability entirely. While I sit and am typing along on my computer writing, or when I am out doing a talk or presentation, I totally forget about being unable, limited, dependent, and incapable. These are common feelings I have when I am out in society and even at home. If I am home and want to clean a closet (trust me, it is out of need), I quickly think of all the help I will require, making me feel dependent. I cannot lift boxes, move clothes easily, or reach high. When I decide to make tamales for the holidays, I feel incapable. Not because I don't know what to do, but because, even in my kitchen that I have made as accessible as can be, there are still barriers that make me need help. Out in society, barriers, or people themselves, remind me of what I am unable to do.

However, give me a keyboard or an audience, then, I do it all on my own. I am not an expert in anything except one thing and that is MY LIFE. So, I am confident that no one else can write about my life like I can. Additionally, I think that the thirty years of experience as an educator made me a skilled teacher. I love sharing what I know. Just like any strategy, some of my ideas may work; some may not. However, I feel satisfied if I know that what I wrote or what I said changed someone in a positive way. So, work ends up being my escape from reality, especially because my disability becomes an asset.

And though most individuals with disabilities, including myself, do not want to be seen as "inspirational" for simply rolling around, I accept being considered motivational when I share my life. It is encouraging to know that I motivate others to look at their own lives differently. So instead of thinking of myself as inspirational, I think the best word for it is *motivational*. I want people to be motivated. I want individuals to use their talents for their own good and the good of others. Many of my students were motivated because they saw themselves in me. When I was a student, I was also motivated when I met other professionals who were Latinos and individuals with disabilities. It gave me hope, and I admired what success looked like.

I used my disability as a tool to motivate students who needed that extra push. One example comes to mind. A student, Matt, became quadriplegic due to an auto accident. He came to me, full of anger about what had happened and how his life had drastically changed. As we built rapport, we developed a trusting connection. One winter day, when he came for his appointment, it was evident that he was having a difficult day. He complained about how some of the sidewalks had not been shoveled. He said, "Sometimes I wish I had died in the accident instead of having to be in a wheelchair." He quickly realized what he had said and tried to take his words back. However, I was not offended. But instead, I used my own disability as a tool to "fill his tank" with motivation.

First, I said, "Matt, you did not offend me. Thank you for feeling comfortable enough with me to tell me your true feelings." I think he was a little surprised that I didn't become defensive or angry. I went on to say, "The wheelchair is not what frustrated you. What frustrated you was that the sidewalks were not clean, creating a barrier for you. I will make sure to ask the appropriate people to remedy that." My comment gave him permission to stress how his wheelchair made everything harder. I responded, "Yes, life can be more challenging, but it is not enough for wanting to die. I am in a wheelchair, and I still have a full and happy life. I have an education and a career I love. I am married and have two beautiful daughters. I own my own home and I drive. I can afford my cost of living and even have a little extra money to vacation and have fun. My life is worth living, and so is yours!"

Matt continued working with me, and that honest, direct conversation motivated him to make the best of his new life. Yes, his life had changed. But a life change is never a reason to want to give up and die. To this day, though it has been many years since our interaction, we remain in contact. His mother calls me at times, even now that I am retired. His mom always wanted to show her appreciation, regularly bringing in treats that I would then share with the entire department. She often told me that she would never forget all that I did to help her son. During one of our conversations, I received the greatest compliment I had ever received. With a smile, she said, "Thank you. I may have given Matt life, but your example and support brought him back to life."

Keeping a constant level of motivation is easier when what we are doing what matters to us. That has been my case. If I had to do math all day, I would likely give up and quit or, at the minimum, struggle to keep my motivation. But because I love teaching, writing, and speaking, I am motivated to keep doing a good job. I always told my students not to decide on careers based on the amount of money they hoped to make but rather to choose a career in fields they loved and would enjoy doing. Sometimes students decided that making a lot of money was most important. I assured them that in the long run, they would probably end up making more money by doing what they loved because they would persist and not give up. As the common saying says, "If you love what you do, you'll never work a day in your life."

A big killer of motivation is fear. I met so many students over the years who got used to failure. Some even admitted to me that they were afraid of being successful, so they didn't even try. I saw many students self-sabotage their success by missing a class for no reason when there was a test. It was much easier for them to fail because they knew what was going to happen. If they succeeded, they were afraid of not knowing what to do. Most of all, they were afraid of succeeding and then not being able to maintain the good grades. Students would say, "it's too much work" or "it won't matter how I do; I have failed so many classes already." I never formed any judgment or fed into their own self-defeating thoughts. I believed in them. And I was often rewarded when students learned that I was right in believing in them. Success feels much better than failure, so the effort and motivation is well worth it.

What is sad is that students who have legitimate reasons for struggles lose their motivation due to the reaction of others and, quite frankly, due to our educational system. When someone fails, there are quick judgments attributing their failure to lack of effort or not being motivated. Students are judged and told that they should increase their motivation, try harder, or worse, they are made to believe that they are not smart enough to succeed. Sometimes, the motivation is there, but it may be lost because of difficulties caused by an undiagnosed disability, living in an abusive home, or having other similar life challenges. Faculty who built relationships with students were able to help by determining the real reason for failure.

Our educational system, whether we admit it or not, classifies students based on their performance on academic or standardized testing. They are classified a certain way, and then the student keeps that classification until they graduate from high school. My two daughters are only seven months apart in age. They have always been in the same grades, although never in the same classroom per my request. Starting in the early grades, each of my daughters was put on a different "assembly line" as I call it. Ariana was placed in the line leading students to college. On the other hand, Ariel was in a different line, which directed students to work. From second grade on, there were already predictions of their success. Each one of my daughters belonged to a different line, even when the motivation was the same between them.

Of course, I didn't agree with putting them in different categories with different expectations. I knew that Ariel had difficulties, but I realized there had to be a reason for her struggles, since lack of motivation was not one of them. Someone who isn't motivated would want to miss school or wouldn't be excited about going to school in general. Ariel didn't miss school and she liked school during her first years. She always attempted to do her homework, and as I assisted her, I noticed that she had legitimate difficulties. She tried hard but couldn't sound out the words to be able to read them. I had been right; because of my insistence, she was later diagnosed with anxiety and learning disabilities in language.

What is sad to me is that, because of her difficulties, she was not encouraged or motivated to consider college. They put her on a track that was entirely different from Ariana's. I remember how upsetting it was for Ariel to receive the "yellow envelope" at the end of the school year, instead of the "white envelope" like her sister. This was the system the school used to indicate the type of letter the student would get to take home. The "yellow envelope" signified that summer school was highly encouraged. Those with the "white envelope," like Ariana, were not encouraged to go to summer school. Students are smart and they quickly learned exactly what the envelopes meant. If the use of the different color envelopes was to keep confidentiality, that plan failed because students figured out who was smart and who wasn't anyway. They knew that getting a yellow envelope signified that they weren't smart and therefore had to go to summer school.

When they were juniors in high school, each of my daughters received different treatment based on the "assembly line" they were in. Ariana could have wallpapered her room with college applications and invitations to different college-preparatory events. Ariel, on the other hand, received only one. She received Triton's application, since that is our district community college. I am sure this affected Ariel's motivation and made her think college was not for her. However, Ariana was solicited, and schools were fighting to have her because she was a top student academically.

It seems ironic that the students who needed more encouragement got none. It didn't matter the reasons for her difficulties. The only thing that mattered were her grades. This quickly led Ariel to lose her motivation, figuring that college was not for her. She was just living up to the schools' expectations. And, of course, isn't it silly to require summer school for the students who may not like school because of their difficulties? I understand that this is in an effort to improve her academic skills; as an educator, I know the intent. But as a mother, I was able to observe and experience the reality through Ariel's faltering self-esteem.

We must motivate all students. We must motivate our children. The more we encourage students to seek out what motivates them, the more they are going to develop the grit to get through their difficulties. As educators, we must motivate all students, not just our stellar ones. Those students are already motivated. As parents, we must accept our children's strengths and difficulties, and above all, we must demonstrate that we believe in them. The more that we voice our expectations of success, the more that they will know we believe in them. Equally important is to find the support and strategies that will help them navigate their difficulties.

Life is full of reasons to give up. We need to make sure that we, as parents, teachers, friends, and community members, are not one of them. Additionally, we can't let others define our futures or limit our potential for success. We are our own writers of our life journeys. Children need to learn that success belongs to everyone. We need to remind them that every single person has a purpose in life and that they must believe in their own potential just as much as in the potential of every other human being. Most of all, we must look for sources of motivation and help our children to do the same. Motivation is what will get us through each bump in the road.

REFLECTION QUESTIONS

1. What helps you keep your motivation?
2. What makes you lose your motivation?
3. How do you motivate others?
4. What have you noticed eliminates the motivation of students/children?

CHAPTER 14

NEED

THE BEAUTY OF LIFE IS THAT WE ALL NEED EACH OTHER AT ONE TIME OR another. I do not care who the person is, at one time or another, every individual will need assistance or support from others. I used to hate being dependent and often needing others to help me. However, as I matured and was able to help others, I changed my perspective. I discovered that, just like I often need others, others have needed me. Need unites us and makes us work together in partnership.

The level of need varies depending on a person's life circumstances, but everyone needs something. People are sometimes born in situations where they may not have their essential basic needs met. Some don't have the privilege of having a roof over their heads, or food, or safety. Although my parents always had a roof over our heads and at least rice and beans to eat on the table, they experienced lack of resources, particularly medical care for me when we lived in Mexico. This is one of the main reasons why they made the difficult decision to immigrate to Chicago. The need was greater than any fear of the unknown. They wanted medical treatment for me because of my diagnosis of polio and because they didn't otherwise have access to medical treatment or medical equipment to help me with my mobility. They knew they needed to do something when they saw me scooting around on the ground because I couldn't move my legs; they knew I wouldn't have much of a future without this sacrifice.

Need is all relative. When our family of eleven first moved to Chicago into a two-bedroom home, we felt like the richest people on earth. Yet we quickly learned that we were considered a low-income status family who was "in need." Because of our status, we qualified for financial assistance for my medical care. Accepting support was difficult for my parents. They were proud people and never wanted to depend on the government for anything. My parents accepted the help only because it was explained to them that the social agencies, such as the March of Dimes and Easter Seals, helped many families with resources collected through donations. Because of my dad's strong ethic, he always donated whatever he could to many of the same organizations that once had supported our family.

Pride often gets in the way of people asking for help even when they need it. In the previous chapter on motivation, I shared how there are things that I cannot do, like cleaning a closet, because of the physical demands it requires. When the weather starts to get better and I need to put my winter clothes away and replace them with my summer clothes, I need assistance. Although I know I need help, it is never easy to acknowledge that we cannot do something on our own and that we depend on the help of others. One year, I asked my sister for help, and when she came over to my house to help me, I started to complain, saying, "I am useless! I cannot even organize a closet without some help." She stopped what she was doing and said, "What do you mean? You are not useless. Look at all you do. I cannot even make a doctor's appointment because of my limited English. Now that is useless in comparison." My sister made a good point. We typically compensate for what we lack with other things we can do. It's easy to forget and lose sight of our strengths because we are too busy focusing on our weaknesses.

What's amazing is that sometimes we get more than what we expected when we extend a helping hand to someone in need. I made it my mission to help my students, and what I've received back has been more than I ever thought was possible. I am who I am because of my students and how we mutually learned from and helped each other. No matter who the person is, they can help and meet the needs of someone else. Sometimes my students with more significant limitations helped professors without knowing it. Many professors grew professionally as teachers through experiences with students with disabilities that challenged them. Though the students might have believed that they were the needy ones and the only ones receiving support, they were also helping their professors.

Jon was a student with autism who I met during the first-year experience class I taught. He was highly intelligent, and his interest was history. He was able to read an entire history textbook in a week, remembering in detail everything he read. Some of his professors would call our office for assistance, sharing that sometimes Jon would correct them when they made a mistake or misspoke in class. The student knew the material inside and out, but because of his autism and lack of social skills, he didn't know that correcting a professor in front of everyone was inappropriate. Jon was constantly reminded that interrupting his professors when they were speaking was something he had to stop doing.

In addition to being supported with his inappropriate classroom behavior, Jon was also trying to figure out the best path with his interest in History. Many students who major in history end up becoming history teachers. It was unlikely that Jon would be able to teach, due to his difficulties with communication and lack of understanding of appropriate social behaviors. Though he could understand and memorize the subject matter, his other difficulties wouldn't allow him to succeed in teaching. Jon considered other fields but wondered how he would do at a university where there wouldn't be the type of support he was getting at Harper. However, one of his professors saw his talent and offered him an independent study class where Jon could assist him with research.

Jon was a hit! His professor was so impressed with the quality of Jon's work and with his ability to connect with anything he read related to history. The professor was shocked with just how quickly Jon absorbed so many details from his research. They developed a mutual relationship where they each met each other's needs. Not only that, but because of the relationship between them, the professor took Jon under his wing and even went as far as finding a program that Jon could pursue at a university. Even after Jon transferred, I would regularly see him on campus because the professor kept working with Jon while the professor still received support for his research projects. Before my retirement, the professor informed me that Jon completed his bachelor's in history and that they remained friends. The professor was attempting to help Jon find a paying job. They were both fortunate to have found each other, and each of them fulfilled a need for one another.

Another professor I worked with also developed a great relationship with one of my students. Jessica was a quadriplegic who was taking classes for self-enrichment. Her health was uncertain, and her father just wanted to give Jessica a college experience. She was very interested in art, but we had to figure out a way that she would be able to draw with her limited mobility in her arms and hands. A professor took it upon himself to try to figure out a solution. He used materials he had at home to develop a desktop that could be placed on top of the drawing table. The desktop included Velcro ties that could easily and safely be used to fasten her hands so that they would not fall off the table when she drew. It was incredible to see how a professor found possibilities for what seemed impossible. He was willing to help meet Jessica's needs by being creative. As a result of this, the professor developed a close relationship with Jessica and her family. Unfortunately, not too long ago, the professor informed me that the student had passed away and that he had been there when she took her last breath. What an incredible story that shows the power of helping others by addressing needs. Not only did she enjoy art, but I am sure that Jessica's life was significantly improved because of the professor's ingenious support.

When we all look around us, we will find someone who is in desperate need, even when we think we have nothing to offer. As a person with a physical disability, I cannot offer much in terms of physical support. But I can certainly offer myself as a person to talk to and especially as a person to pray. My friends know that I am here for them and they can call upon me to support them. Sometimes all a person needs is a smile when they are feeling down. At times, what is of most importance doesn't cost us a dime. We can all offer a smile freely.

In helping professions, when we see so many people in need, it can be exhausting. Compassion fatigue is real, because sometimes even with all our desire to meet a need, we are not able to successfully support every person in the way we want. Time, resources, and the person's willingness to be supported can all be unbreakable barriers in aiding a person in need. I know that there were times when I had to meet my own needs first before I could continue helping. When I was feeling this way, I gave myself permission to have a personal mental health day. It is important to be aware of our own feelings and attend to them as soon as possible. If we do not help ourselves, how can we expect to be able to help others?

I worked in the same role for thirty years, a difficult job because students were dealing with not only their disabilities, but also with difficult life situations. People would ask me how I didn't burn out. My response was easy: I loved what I was doing, and I saw it as my mission to help my students. What is interesting, however, is that I was very much like my mother in how I supported my students. I never felt sorry for them. I always held them accountable and made them see their own self-worth. I reprimanded them, in a kind, gentle way, when I needed to for the sake of the students' growth. Sometimes my coworkers observed how I interacted with my students and were shocked that they always came back, even with my direct approach. I was real. I was not there to handhold. I had expectations of each of them.

Sometimes I used strategies that were less than typical. I had a student, Eddie, who didn't do much school work outside the classroom. Together we created a plan around his job where he could do some schoolwork. During one of our appointments, I asked if he had done his reading for a psychology class he was taking. He said he had. I asked him if he could show me his psychology book. He pulled it out and handed it to me. Immediately, I noticed that the book was cold, as if it had been left in a cold car. I said, "Eddie, your book seems cold. Why is it so cold?" I guess he didn't have time to make up an explanation because he said, "Oh, sorry,

I didn't do my reading. My book was left in the car all weekend." I thought to myself, "I can now add something new to my job description—taking the temperature of books."

We sometimes are quick to judge whether a person is in need when we see them begging for money in the middle of the streets. In the instant of a red light, we process the situation and decide whether to help or not. Typically, I respond by quickly giving them any loose change in my cup holder. Although I may make quick judgments and question why they are not working and instead opt to ask for donations, I decide to give them money anyway. I am fully aware that life situations can change instantly, forcing someone out of a safe home. Although they may seemingly look able-bodied, at least compared to me, I know that there are different types of needs. The person may have lost a job or can't find one because they don't have an address, which is usually required on an application. Or the person may be dealing with psychological or other types of invisible disabilities. Perhaps the person may lack literacy skills because of not having educational opportunities. I will never know the truth. All I know is that the spare change I give is not much and that I wouldn't even miss it. What the person does with it or why the person is even begging should not matter to me.

Just like I may judge the person who begs and seems to be able to work, I have been judged as a person in need because I use a wheelchair. We used to laugh when I took my girls out trick-or-treating when they were young, because I would return with more loot than they did. During the holidays, if I went out shopping, sometimes I'd be offered money, by complete strangers, for my Christmas purchases. It was always an awkward situation to have to tell them that I didn't need the money. Having a disability makes us look needy. Sometimes I even wondered if I was better off financially than those who wanted to give me money.

It is important to be aware of the reason we decide to give. I try not to ever give because of pity. I don't like to be pitied so I try not to pity others either. Once, when I was in New Mexico at a conference, I observed many individuals begging near the convention center. I saw a woman with two little ones holding a bucket for donations. My heart strings were pulled, and I started to feel sorry for them, especially the children. However, I stopped myself and shifted to thoughts about what I could do to help. I decided to go to a nearby McDonalds and I purchased a meal for the mother and two Happy Meals for the children. When I did this, the woman was very touched. She thanked me, and it was clear she was surprised that a disabled woman was helping her. I felt better knowing that I provided a meal rather than just formulating my own story about her life that would cause me to pity them.

Of course, I will never know the story behind every person I support financially, but I hope that any contribution helps them at least with the most basic need—food. It is unfortunate that sometimes I choose not to give because of fear of my own safety. I would love to live in a world where people would not have to be out in the streets begging and others would not have to be afraid of being caring and helping. I think this is a societal issue that, if we worked together, we could address. I know it's a dream, but one that I can do my part in making come true.

Food insecurity is real, and it can happen to any of us. At Harper, though it is located in an affluent community, students I worked with sometimes suffered from food insecurity. I was so glad to see that Harper made strides to address this by providing resources for a pantry that could help students. Students were able to go in and pick up a snack or other personal basic things like soap, toothbrushes, etc. In my office, I made sure to keep my own collection of snacks to offer students. I even had a mini refrigerator where I could not only keep my lunch but also keep other foods and drinks to offer students if they were ever hungry.

Perhaps because my parents shared many stories of the poverty they experienced as children, I am extra sensitive to people who may be hungry. I have never experienced hunger, but my parents did. Likewise, my daughters have never experienced hunger, so sometimes I am concerned that they may take food for granted. I regularly reprimand my daughters when they are wasteful. Sometimes they take a bite of a sandwich and then decide that they don't want it anymore. They are quick to want to throw the bitten sandwich in the trash. I remind them that food should never be wasted and suggest they save it to eat it later. In my opinion, it seems that each generation gets more wasteful than the previous. If we don't experience hunger, we take having food for granted.

The bottom line is that need exists in all of us. We will depend on each other at one time or another. Also, we are all able to help when someone is in need. It is reciprocal, uniting us in one more way as humans. We are here in life together, wanting the same things. We want our basic needs met. It is up to each of us to be there for one another. I do something for a neighbor today, and tomorrow a neighbor does something for me. It was meant to be this way.

REFLECTION QUESTIONS

1. What do you do to meet the needs of others?
2. How have others helped you with your needs?
3. Are there things that you can do to meet the needs of someone you do not know?

CHAPTER 15

OPPORTUNITIES

IN MEXICO, ALTHOUGH I LIVED A HAPPY CHILDHOOD, I WOULD HAVE never gotten the opportunities that the United States has offered me. I can't predict what my life would have been like, but I know that I wouldn't have been as successful as I have been in this country. The resources were just not there. Would I have lived to be the age I am today had I remained in Mexico? What would have been the quality of my life had my parents not immigrated to the US? I know it is probably silly to dwell on these questions, but sometimes it helps me be even more grateful for the sacrifices my parents made when we moved to Chicago. Without knowing what the future would hold, they brought us to a foreign land with the hopes of a better life, which fortunately we do now have.

Regularly I wonder if the American Dream, which is why most immigrants move here from their countries, really exists. Are all people offered the same opportunities? I used to think that we were, but that some people took advantage of them while others did not. However, as I deeply reflect on opportunities, I have concluded that not everyone is offered the same chances for success. I am sure some would argue with this opinion. Some would even be surprised that I believe this, especially because the odds were against me, yet with the opportunities I received, I come close to what people consider living the American Dream.

I have met many people from all walks of life. Some are very successful and wealthy economically. Some are homeless and suffer food insecurity. Many are like me. I am not wealthy, but I certainly do not experience food insecurity. Is this because the wealthy person had more opportunities? What is the explanation for the disparity in how people live? Perhaps at a different stage of my life, I would have said that we all received the same opportunities but that our wealth is derived from whether we took those opportunities or not. However, I now believe that the opportunities are never the same.

Sure, I totally believe that hard work is required for success most of the time. However, how different is the experience of someone who has all the resources to get an education? Certainly, not every student who wants to go to college is offered the opportunity to do so. Many could never enter a college classroom if it weren't for the financial aid and scholarships that are available for students within a certain income level. And still, some students are not even eligible to receive aid or scholarships because of their immigration status, giving them even fewer opportunities. Many individuals can attend college without any worry about how it will be financed. And then there are people like me that worked hard and accepted every opportunity that I was offered to get an education.

Opportunities depend on different things. It may depend on where people are born, their race, or their gender. Sometimes it also depends on which family a person is born into. For example, I was born into a very supportive, cohesive family who always gave me love and encouragement. Not everyone has this experience. Additionally, a person's health is another factor that influences opportunities. I was born in Mexico, so the opportunities my parents had to treat my polio were different than if I had been born in the United States. However, even in this country, because of my race, I may not have received the same opportunities as others. Because I am a female, this too, affected the types of opportunities I had, even more so in my culture.

I acknowledge that I was fortunate to have been born to a family who loved me and provided me with security, whereas others are born into single parent households or broken homes, limiting them from the same opportunities I had. A polio diagnosis also changed the opportunities I would have in life. An able-bodied person has more opportunities because they live in a world that is made for them. On the other hand, I must constantly battle the stigma that comes with having a disability, on top of all the accessibility barriers I must navigate.

Even with the disparate opportunities people receive, though, it is important to take the opportunities when they come. I know that we are all guilty of making judgments about others based on our belief that opportunities are given to everyone equally but that some prefer to take the easy route. Opportunities do require effort, but we cannot assume that the opportunities are equal for everyone. For example, as a child I had the opportunity to learn English because of attending school. My mother didn't have this opportunity because her priorities had to be different. She was a stay-at-home mom who watched all of us. So, to believe that she did not learn English because of not acting on an opportunity would be wrong.

Similarly, my father also didn't have the same opportunities to learn English as I did. Although he worked outside the home, his factory hired primarily Spanish-speaking employees. All he ever heard was Spanish. For someone who never went to school, though, I was quite impressed with his knowledge of different materials, especially with his English skills. He was able to understand all conversations and even spoke some English, although not as proficient as he wanted.

I had many Latino students with similar situations; their parents never learned to speak English. Some people will find it easy to say that they could have attended school to learn English, but we can't be so quick to judge without understanding what is going on in people's lives. Because of limited English and perhaps a minimal education, parents struggle to support their children financially and educationally. How can they support their students, the way they want, when they make minimum wages, and they are unfamiliar with the college experience?

Many first-generation college students must fend for themselves without the support of their families, just like I did. This sets them apart from their classmates who get support from their college-educated parents. These different levels of support clearly will affect the students' opportunities. Some students may miss out on important information because they do not have a family member directing them. Had it not been for me finding the support from a Latina professional at DePaul, I may have missed many opportunities that put me on the path for success. I was too busy trying to stay on track with grades, so having someone helping me was crucial.

Grades also affect a person's opportunities. And grades are not always based on effort like many believe. When I was preparing to go to law school, it was encouraged that students take a Law School Admission Test (LSAT) preparatory course. The class was costly, and financial aid would not cover the expense. I couldn't afford the course, so I had to study twice as hard on my own, whereas some of my friends who had the financial means took the course. I did well, but I wonder how I would have done had I taken the preparatory course. A better score could have changed some of the opportunities I was offered.

One thing I am sure of is that opportunities do not come looking for us. We must go out and find them. Sometimes, people may not even recognize an opportunity when they see it, believing that they do not deserve it or are embarrassed to act on it. Accurate information is necessary to know when there is an opportunity. And even then, some people do not know where to access it. Culture and language may play a part in whether a person knows about an opportunity and whether they act on it or not.

For this reason, I worked hard in informing my students of any opportunities available for them. Both Latino students and students with disabilities need additional support in finding all that is available, especially when their parents may not have the information to help. I also encouraged my students to get involved in clubs and organizations on campus. Many of the opportunities I found when I was a student were by word of mouth from other students who were in a similar life situation as I was. Developing relationships and networking helps tremendously in keeping informed.

As a new author, I learned a lot about the publishing business because I had the time after I retired. Previously, I, like many people, thought getting published was too difficult, therefore making the goal seemingly unattainable. I had never contemplated the idea of self-publishing as an option, assuming that it was very difficult and costly. Now I am aware that goals often seem impossible until we find the right information and/or encouragement from others. I wish I had learned all that I know now about publishing long ago since I love writing. I probably could have published several books long ago if I had had the information. Being home during the pandemic gave me the time to do research to find the necessary information and opportunities. I also used connections I had made to get the best information. Now, I want to share my knowledge and encouragement with others. Through my experience with publishing, I have met different people who are also interested in publishing, and I gladly offer my support.

Opportunities are out there, but sometimes they are not readily accessible. Sometimes, we might not even know where to look or who to ask. If we don't know what opportunities are out there, then how can we take advantage of them? Again, language is a big barrier for many people. Although things are changing, most of the time the information about opportunities is in English, so many Latinos are not aware of what is out there. Fortunately, I am noticing more attempts to have information available in different languages.

Additionally, there are groups that want to provide support to those who may need information about opportunities for their children. Recently, I attended a Bilingual Summit. I was so happy to see so many parent groups gathered to discuss important topics that impact the children of their families. I attended the summit to co-present with members of the Mannheim School District 83 Bilingual Parent Advisory Council (BPAC). Our presentation was to showcase the wonderful work of this group, including their process in writing their own vignettes for publishing in the near future. This group of parents have invited me to several of their meetings. I love how the group is involved and participates in events that affect their students and the community. I joke and tell them that I am happy they adopted me. Without groups like this, students would not have the advocates they need to ensure that they have access to the same opportunities that other students have.

I have also used my personality to my advantage to help me find more opportunities. I am not afraid to ask questions, connect with people, make calls, and do research to find my answers. My daughters, as smart as they are, do not have the same kind of personality, so they are timid in taking the initiative to ask questions to find opportunities. Fortunately, as an educator, and with my personality, I can share information about opportunities they might benefit from. For example, I encouraged Ariana to apply for an academic scholarship given at Harper. She was one of four recipients, and the $10,000 she won was very helpful to offset the cost of her tuition.

Some people do not pay attention to important communications because they are constantly bombarded with information that makes them confused about what even pertains to them. With the multitude of information that comes through to our email accounts, it is easy to overlook an opportunity. Recently, Facebook sent an email to all its users regarding a class action lawsuit. Every member of my family has an account and received the email. If we wanted to be a part of the class action lawsuit, all we had to do was to complete a form. I was the only one in my family who read the email and submitted the form. Because of this, I received close to $400 as restitution. Isidro remembers seeing the email, but he thought it was spam.

The most important opportunity we have is to make our lives better. This opportunity is available for everyone equally. The power is all ours, and this is the most important opportunity in anyone's life. It is a matter of looking at our lives, reflecting, and making the changes we need to improve our lives. Our lives will be improved if we take the opportunity to change our attitudes and to be more loving with ourselves and others. Our lives will dramatically improve if we take the opportunity to have courage over our fears. We will greatly benefit if we learn to understand the differences between people. Equally as important, we must take each opportunity and put in the effort to accomplish our goals. Other opportunities that may enhance the quality of our lives can include living with faith, appreciating all of our blessings, laughing a little more, always nurturing our intelligence, trying to be just in all we do, being loyal to ourselves and others, staying motivated in meeting our goals, and helping the needy. The quality of our life depends entirely on us. It is up to each of us to act on this most important opportunity.

REFLECTION QUESTIONS

1. What opportunities have helped you succeed in life?
2. What opportunity would have helped you in life?
3. How do you respond to unexpected opportunities?
4. How do you encourage your children/others to find opportunities?

CHAPTER 16

PRESENT

To be happy in life, sometimes we must let go of the past, be grateful for what we have, and look forward to what is yet to come. If we do not let go of the past, it might destroy our today. The present is what we have now, yet we always prefer to think of the past and/or the future. Certainly, reflecting on the past is important so we can learn from our mistakes and grow. Thinking of the future can also be beneficial because, in life, we need to have goals to achieve what we aspire. However, we should not live our lives wishing to change the past. What has happened already cannot be changed. Likewise, it is not fruitful to get hung up on the past or the future, losing sight of what matters most—today.

Sometimes the greatest miracles happen unexpectedly, but we miss them because our minds may be burdened by hurt, resentment, or anger over something that already happened in the past. We lose sight of how useless it is to dwell on something we cannot alter. Unfortunately, we typically look at the past not to learn from our mistakes or to make amends with people we may have hurt, but instead, we look at the past because of regret, and we get stuck focusing on what can no longer be changed. When we do this, instead of helping ourselves, it is counterproductive, and we just end up hurting more.

In the same manner, when we look at the future, it isn't just to remind ourselves of our goals. We focus on the future simply to want to speed up our lives to get to what we predict will happen and be better in our lives. As we all know, the future is not guaranteed. Yet, we live waiting for the next vacation, the next promotion, the next party, or the next deadline for something we really want. I have noticed the various ways people keep a countdown, always wanting something in the future which is not even promised. Is there any benefit in doing that?

Personally, I never struggled or got stuck in the past. Quite the contrary, I opted to forget the past and push down any hurt or pain I suffered. I strategically did this because my past caused hurt and disappointment. It wasn't until recently that I took the time to reflect on my past. It was very therapeutic for me because I chose to look at the past as an affirmation that I have come a long way. By looking at my past, I was able to publish my first book, a memoir. In this book I retell my story—the good, the bad, and the ugly. It was painful to recall everything that I overcame. Interestingly, I thought that I had forgotten my past, but I discovered that I had just suppressed all the hurt so that I could continue. Through the process of reflecting on my past, though, I concluded that there wasn't only hurt in my life. There were many happy and funny moments that made my life interesting and molded me into the woman I am today.

It is amazing the level of detail I remembered from different parts of my life. All along, I thought that the memories were gone, but I recollected everything that happened to me. Yes, I cried recounting parts of what I endured in my life. But mostly, I celebrated knowing that I survived and that I am still here. So, looking at my past served a purpose. I used it to grow and to become stronger. I jokingly say that I've discovered that I have a unique type of amnesia. I forgot the pain but remembered the gain. If we looked at our past with this type of amnesia, then looking at our past would be worthwhile.

Somehow, this is not how most people look at their past. In my job, I developed relationships with many students who struggled to let go of the past. No matter how much I reminded them that life doesn't have to necessarily be based on past experiences, they brought the baggage with them. We have the power to change, to grow, and to be happy. Some students came to Harper without any hope, clinging to their past difficulties in school. They predicted that they would have the same experiences again. Sometimes I had to work very hard to get students to believe in their own potential. They were accustomed to failure since it was what they had experienced in their past schools.

Mary is a student who allowed her past to impact her chances for success. She not only had learning disabilities but also had a history of substance abuse. Although she was clean when she started seeing me, she constantly remembered her past, often shutting the door to any possibility for success. She didn't believe in herself and felt that, at any time, she could become the same person who would hang out with friends to do drugs so that they could forget their pain. I wanted her to recognize her courage and to focus on moving forward one step at a time. The past was such a hindrance in her being able to see present time, much less a bright future. I worked with her patiently, celebrating each success, using them as proof that she could start a new chapter in her life.

One day, Mary came into my office and was gleaming with joy. She said, "Pascuala, I did it! I passed the test I was so afraid of taking." She struggled immensely with test taking, admitting that most of the time when she took tests in the past, she was high because she used drugs to calm her anxiety. At Harper she did not know how she would handle taking tests without the use of drugs. I smiled and asked if I could give her a hug! I then commented, "I knew you could do it. I hope you now know that you can get through anything without relying on drugs. It is all up to you to leave the past in the past." She smiled back and said, "Baby steps." That was a phrase I often used with her to motivate her and allow her to see that with baby steps she could get very far. Sometimes, our past is cruel and holds us back as prisoners. It is up to us to find the key to loosen our chains. Once opened, we should throw away the key so that we could start fresh.

Though I have been successful at leaving the past in the past, I do struggle with worrying too much about the future. I am the type of person who is always counting days. I would have countdowns at work all the time. A friend and coworker, Michele, tried to help me to live the day without rushing time away. She had a point. I was spending too much time thinking of a future date that was supposed to bring me happiness. I counted days before the holidays. I counted days before our winter break or summer break as if thinking that those times would be better. I'd start my countdowns a few weeks ahead of time, marking down each day as it passed. And when the date came, I was expecting a different type of experience, but it was all the same. I would then start a new countdown. All the while, I was missing the important moments that were occurring around me daily.

Now I realize that I should have been celebrating each day without wanting to hurry up the clock. Michele was so right in telling me to not speed up my days. It is funny that this has remained a joke between us. I no longer have work-related countdowns, but now she does. Although we no longer work together, she knows I am very familiar with the yearly school schedule at Harper. I get occasional texts from her saying, "Twelve more days until summer." I just laugh and appreciate how her words have stuck with me, and it is hilarious how she has started her own countdowns. Now, I try not to have as many countdowns, though sometimes I can't help myself. Of course, I am a list maker and hyper-organized with my calendar, so I sometimes fall back on my old bad habits. However, I keep Michele's wise advice tucked away and regularly go back to it.

Thinking of the future is helpful at times because it makes us think of our goals and the future we want to create. I always had students develop short-term and long-term goals. However, I would always remind them that unless they put action to the goal, the goal would never be a reality. Thinking of the future can also be a source of motivation. It is unrealistic not to have hopes for what we want in our futures. I recently did a presentation using my memoir. I shared that, in my life, I have accomplished many things that would have seemed impossible. I also explained that sometimes

I felt guilty of always wanting more. However, I encouraged the audience to do the same. No matter our age, whether young or more mature, life is only meaningful when we have hopes and aspirations of what we want in our future. Today, I was at a book fair, and I met an eighty-five-year-old woman who was full of spunk. We chatted and, in our conversation, she assured me that she would make it to one hundred years of life. She said, "Fifteen more years? A piece of cake." She even had me feel her biceps to demonstrate how strong she was. That approach to life is what fuels our tank with aspirations and wishes. We should have them until the very last breath we take.

Even though there is a purpose to looking at our past and future, the source of our happiness is in the now. After all, isn't today the only thing we have assured? Yesterday is gone. It will never come back. And tomorrow is not promised or guaranteed. First, there is no assurance that we will have a tomorrow, and second, even if we did, there is no guarantee that our plans will come true. The more that we stay in the now, the happier we will be. We can focus on the small miracles that each day brings. For example, I am sitting in my garden listening to the birds sing. Though the weather is cloudy, I observe how the sun wants to peek through. I look at the array of colors of the flowers in my garden. I just noticed that my tomato plant is taller than I am. I'm noticing that my tree is full of peaches that will ripen before my own eyes. (OK, I am guilty. I took a quick glance at the future by thinking of the delicious peaches I will soon be eating!) Instead of thinking of my past or future, it brought me joy to discover the beauty of today, because I was savoring the present.

Not long ago, I had a strange thought. (Readers are probably noticing this trend!) I woke up and began thinking of what I had planned for the day. Then I thought to myself, each day is like a mystery. I may have planned what I wanted to do. But isn't each day a complete surprise? We try to take control of the day, and sometimes we may even believe we do. But the reality is that there is a mystery to each day. For example, I knew that I had a book fair to attend, but I had no clue that an eighty-five-year-old woman, full of spunk, would chat with me and even give me a massage (she gave all authors a massage) because she did massages as a career before retiring over twenty years previously. What an enjoyable surprise!

Of course, I am careful not to over reflect on how each day is a surprise, because this thinking can lead to anxiety if we let it. Because we do not know what will happen from one minute to the other, we seem to be at the mercy of something. Depending on what we believe, we are at the mercy of destiny, God, or whatever else. I think this is one of the main reasons why I have believed that disability is the marginalized group most discriminated against, ignored, or misunderstood. Perhaps seeing someone with a disability reminds able-bodied people that even the next minute is not guaranteed and that their life could change instantly. Could it be that seeing people with disabilities is a reminder that the person is just a few steps away from having an accident resulting in an injury?

But knowing that each day is a mystery can bring joy too. Just like we may have planned the day, we can also receive beautiful surprises. A few weeks ago, I was going through my day with no spectacular plans. My daughter Ariel, who married in January 2022, came to tell me that she was pregnant. What an unexpected, beautiful surprise. The news filled me with joy and aspirations. I can't help but think of the future when my grandchild joins us in life. The baby is not even born yet, but my heart is full of love already. Because of the news, I had to adjust some of my goals. I was planning to write this book in the winter when the weather is less than pleasant. However, now I would rather play with the new addition to the family in the winter, so I had to change the timeline for my book.

Focusing on today can also help us to make life manageable. On busy weeks, when I have a full calendar of events, I get overwhelmed and stressed with everything that I must get done. But I begin to calm down when I make the decision to take one day at a time, breaking all my obligations into manageable segments. I encouraged students to do the same so that they wouldn't feel swamped with all their assignments that were due. Getting overwhelmed often led to students wanting to give up. It was common for students to start off the semester full of energy, focus, and good intentions, but they began to feel burnt out as the assignments accumulated. I spent time showing them how to use a planner and to even break down projects into smaller chunks. Most students lacked basic study skills, so time management strategies were very necessary.

Above all, focusing on the present can assist us in being more grateful for our lives. Each morning, I thank God for allowing me to wake up to a new day. Thinking only of the day helps us not to take things for granted. Several years ago, I suffered from extreme back pain because of always sitting in my wheelchair. I have had scoliosis, which is the curvature of the spine, for almost as long as I can remember. This curvature was pinching my sciatic nerve. I was miserable and thought I was going to need a surgical intervention. My back was in pain all the time. It would hurt even more each time my wheelchair bounced because of a sidewalk bump. Fortunately, my brother Lalo knew of a masseuse who had helped him in the past. Because his business had stairs, he agreed to come to my house for the massage. At that point, I would have done anything to alleviate the pain.

After several massages, miraculously my back didn't hurt anymore. He used acupuncture and hot cupping on my back. I was so grateful to have found a remedy for all the pain I was experiencing. I share this story because since that experience, I appreciate each day without back pain. When I wake up and can move without pain, I take the time to thank God. It is so easy to complain without appreciating that we are healthy and pain free. Remembering to appreciate each day that we are healthy is a practice I plan to always follow. Perhaps because of my vulnerability due to my disability, I am so grateful when I do not experience pain during the day.

Sometimes, our thoughts take over and control us. Without realizing it, we might be going to our past even when it brings us pain. We use the future to plan what we cannot control, and then get mad when things do not go our way. With effort, we can control our thoughts so that they go to what really matters. Living each day fully will bring more joy. Regretting our past or aspiring to a future that may not come may bring unhappiness and anxiety. Today, just today! Let's be grateful for today!

REFLECTION QUESTIONS

1. When you think of the past, how does it hurt or benefit you?
2. When you think of the future, how does it hurt or benefit you?
3. How does thinking of the present affect your life?

CHAPTER 17
QUIET

In full disclosure, this is an area of my life I need to cultivate. I am not good with quiet! In all honesty, I am awful at being in the quiet. I could blame it on the fact that when I got polio, I was in complete paralysis for six months. Upon waking from my paralysis, perhaps I felt I had had enough quiet. Now, I feel that I cannot stop so I am all over the place and can't stay still. Or I can blame it on my personality, wanting to always be with others. Or I can blame it on being born into a huge family and always being surrounded by people. Regardless of why, I don't practice quietness and this is something I want to change. Our lives need quiet at times.

Since I can remember, I have had people in my life at all times of my day. As I reflect, the only time I was ever alone was during my commute to work, for bathroom/showers, and whenever I was in the hospital. Other than that, I am always with someone—family, friends, or strangers. Even when I write, I must be around sounds, noise, people, TV, or some other type of activity. Quietness is foreign to me, but I know it is very valuable.

I have friends who have shared how much they appreciate quiet. At work when I used to tell my coworkers that, for any given family event, we would have over eighty people there, they couldn't understand what that would be like for them. For Christmas, when my parents were still living, the entire family, which consists of my siblings, their spouses, and their children, would gather in my mom's two-bedroom ranch home. Now that they have passed away, my brother Mon has continued the tradition. For Thanksgiving, we often gathered to make tamales, enough to last us for the long winter. There is always a birthday, a shower, a wedding, or a "just because" gathering that involves the entire family.

All this family activity has not hindered me from reflecting on my life, getting my work done, and doing everything else I need to accomplish. I am the queen multitasker, though I am aware that research shows that this is not a healthy approach. I don't doubt that I might become more effective if I took advantage of some quiet time to focus. I even recommended a quiet and distraction-free environment for my students because I knew how important it was for their concentration. However, I still have not been able to embrace quiet in my own life. Do as I say, not as I do!

Several of my friends practice mindfulness and have encouraged me to try it out. I have never been able to do any of the activities intended to reduce stress such as deep breathing or getting a massage. Just thinking about engaging in any of those kinds of relaxation activities augments my stress instead of reducing it! I don't get many opportunities to be quiet, but I also do not look for them. On the few occasions when I am all alone, I find it difficult and depressing. For some reason my mind always drifts to feeling sad, as if everyone is out there having fun while I am all alone.

Quietness is important, and I know I must experience quiet if I am to truly reflect and cultivate my life. I know the benefits and aspire to practice it more regularly. My husband and my daughter really enjoy being alone. They can get lost reading a good book, thinking, or just doing a quiet activity on their own. I occasionally overhear my husband praying out loud while he is quiet and preparing to end the day. Ariana even bought a t-shirt that's a play on what the Little Mermaid's song says: "I want to be where the people aren't." I have always thought that they liked quiet because they are introverts and that I don't because I'm an extrovert. However, I have never found the real explanation.

Because I understand the value of being in the quiet, when I taught classes, I always included lessons that incorporated meditation and other stress-reducing strategies. When I did, though, I often felt like a hypocrite for teaching what I don't practice. I saw the benefit of teaching these strategies, especially for students who were diagnosed with attention deficit disorders, so it was important for these students to be able to quiet down all the noise that goes on in their heads. Students needed concentration if they were ever to be successful.

Quiet is something I value. Though I do not practice it regularly, when it's forced on me, like when I take a shower or when it's the middle of the night and everyone is asleep, I do my best thinking. Sometimes, when I have a new idea, I hurry up to write down my thoughts because I fear losing them by the time my shower is over or by the time morning comes. When I was writing my memoir, sometimes a story came to mind, and in pitch darkness, I would crank up my laptop so that I could type the story. In the shower, I was known to come up with ideas for programs for the students when I was still working. I just wish I would make quiet time a more regular experience.

As a college student, I coveted quiet because of the amount of schoolwork I had to do. My day was long because, after classes, I preferred to stay on the DePaul University campus to get some studying done. I knew that if I went home, it would be buzzing with noise because my nieces and nephews would be there visiting my mom. I would stay on campus most nights until 10 PM because I knew that by the time I got home, everyone would be off to bed. I then would have a couple of more hours of quiet so that I could concentrate and get my assignments done.

Some of my college students at Harper also struggled with figuring out how to get their school assignments done. I would share what I did when I was a student, suggesting they do the same. We would then strategize the best locations for them to study. This was especially helpful to my Latino students who also had big families. One student even told me that the only quiet place in her home was in the bathroom. Luckily, the campus offered a lot of quiet places for students to use.

Quietness doesn't necessarily mean loneliness. Someone in a noisy room full of people might be lonelier than someone who is all alone in a room. Our lives are full of noise. Children are exposed to endless bells and whistles. The games with more movement, color, and noise are marketed to children as young as three. We are taught to go, go, go, and technology has augmented the need for stimulation. Children are finding it more difficult to entertain themselves with their own creativity. The damage is huge. It is no wonder that each new generation wants things faster, sometimes even immediate, and the louder the better.

When my girls were growing up, I noticed how they enjoyed playing the games that were more interactive and louder. Although we would buy them educational toys, they would often end up being forgotten or going unused. Even when I was trying to put them to sleep, they wanted to hear music. It was difficult to gear them toward games that fostered creativity or critical thinking. They would immediately complain that the toy was too boring.

Quietness can be a personality trait, though most of the time, it is a trait that helps a person from being impulsive and saying something they would regret later. Sometimes I tease both Isidro and Ariana because I can almost hear their brains churning as they're thinking of a response. Unlike me, they carefully choose their words before saying anything, ensuring that they speak clearly and concisely. Sometimes, they prefer to stay quiet and keep their thoughts to themselves. This is something that, in retrospect, could have helped me with the frustration I felt for voicing my opinions and speaking up in situations when it didn't make a difference.

My passion for my job and the students I served prohibited me from remaining quiet, so it was frustrating when I felt that I wasn't being heard. I was always professional and respectful but insisted on advocating for students, even when it was contrary to what the majority wanted to do. After speaking, I sometimes wasn't sure how my comments were perceived. I would ask my colleagues who I trusted, and fortunately, I was always told that I spoke eloquently and straight to the point. Sometimes, I was even thanked for voicing what many of them were thinking but kept to themselves. This approach helped students because I would bring up important issues for discussion. However, I don't doubt that at times it would have been best to remain quiet.

Deciding when to stay quiet and when to speak up is not easy. Of course, it is easy to speak up when there is agreement with the majority. It's not as easy if there is dissent and we are supporting the least-favored opinion. Also, the decision to speak up or not depends on the nature of the discussion, who is in the room, and whether a trusting environment has been established. Sometimes, I took risks, and many were shocked with my frankness.

At times, though, I find quiet without even looking for it. I have recently started gardening, and I have noticed that while I water my many plants, I am most reflective about what is happening in my life. As I roll around, carefully watering each plant, I observe the plant's subtle changes sometimes from one day to the next. I see growth, a new bud, or a wilting flower. During these observations I think a lot about life and how we are all constantly changing just like the flowers do. We all change, and we don't even notice it unless we purposely reflect. Sometimes the changes we go through lead to growth, but other times we need to make more changes because, just like plants, we need to constantly cultivate our lives.

Quietness is the best environment for reflection. Reflecting is the first step toward growth. It is through reflection that we can analyze our lives and make decisions that will lead us closer to living a better life. With reflection we can learn to be at peace with others but most importantly, in quietness we can be at peace with ourselves.

REFLECTION QUESTIONS

1. What do you do for quietness in your life?
2. What have you gained from quietness?
3. Are you comfortable with quietness? Why or why not?

CHAPTER 18

RESOLUTION

RESOLUTIONS SHOULD NOT ONLY HAPPEN WHEN WE ARE SAYING GOODBYE to a year and welcoming a new one. Most people tend to make resolutions then, but resolutions can be part of our lives no matter the year, month, day, or hour. A resolution can be thought of in two ways. First, it can be looked at as what humans resolve to do or a change they plan to implement for improving their lives. Second, a resolution can also be seen as the process of resolving a problem or a discord with another person. In our busy lives, we have many interactions with others, including loved ones. There is no way to entirely escape from disagreements and conflicts within a relationship. What would happen if we didn't try to resolve our problems by coming up with resolutions to our conflicts? The world would be significantly more complicated and chaotic. Friendships would not last; there would be more divorces than there are now; and there could be more violence and disorder.

During the New Year's holiday, traditionally, many of us stay up late and wait to ring in the new year. During this holiday, we say goodbye to the year that is about to end and begin to have hopes for the year that is about to commence. In our minds, we have ideas of what we want to do or change in the new year. However, sometimes we do not have a plan about how to make these ideas or changes possible. This is the time when most people make decisions and plans for the new year but rarely include the step-by-step processes needed to make the resolution possible.

During every New Year holiday, in my family, probably like in other households, we use games to help us think of and voice our resolutions. One silly game we play requires fresh grapes. The idea is to place one grape in our mouth for each resolution made. The goal is to have as many resolutions as possible, which depends on how many grapes fit in our mouths. Resolutions may include goals such as losing weight, finding a new job, cutting back on spending, being more punctual, getting less angry, or other types of specific goals. Of course, it is a fun activity and full of laughs, but often we put more effort in coming up with resolutions that night than actually working on them during the new year.

For some reason, making resolutions brings us comfort because we make a list of things we intend to do or change. However, most people forget about the resolutions they made within a few weeks of the new year. It takes commitment to live up to our resolutions. Honestly, I think the only resolution necessary is that we should always strive to be happy and strive to be the best versions of ourselves for others. Certainly, these resolutions must be part of our everyday lives and not just a game to play on New Year's Eve. Our good intentions may be there, but it is easy to deviate from our intentions and revert to our old habits.

Personally, I have found a method that allows me to keep my resolutions. I have found that if I share a goal or a plan with several people, I will not want to disappoint them, so in a way, they keep me accountable. So, I will not voice a resolution that I don't think I can accomplish. I guess I believe that my word is my honor. If I really want to accomplish something or change in some way, I rely on family and friends to keep me on track. Once I voice what I am intending to do, I am more likely to follow through with my plans.

Just as in goal planning, resolutions must be realistic and doable to avoid setting ourselves up for failure. For example, it would be more realistic to say that ten pounds will be lost during the year versus saying that the resolution is to lose fifty pounds. In the first resolution, if ten or more pounds are lost, it will be a resolution accomplished, making it a reason to celebrate and be proud. On the other hand, in the second example, if only twenty pounds are lost instead of fifty, a person will likely feel disappointed because the resolution was failed, probably negating the great accomplishment. So I have learned to make resolutions that are reachable and realistic for me.

When working with college students with disabilities, I also tried to teach them to make resolutions that made sense for them. A student who struggles academically cannot suddenly become a straight-A student. At the beginning of each semester, as I reviewed their syllabi with them, I would ask what grade they thought they could earn for each class. Of course, they hoped to get an A in each class, but I pointed out that hopes were different than goals. A goal requires them to look at their strengths and weaknesses to determine if the goal will be achievable. I would then direct them to think about their difficulties and would tell them to aim for the grades that they thought were possible. I would remind them that by asserting a certain grade, they were making a commitment to do whatever it took to earn their grade. I even suggested that a goal of a C was appropriate since that would indicate that they successfully passed a course. I'd say, "Just keep your head above C level." Of course, I'd encourage them to try their hardest and if they ended up with higher grades, they would feel even more satisfied.

Resolutions help us from repeating the same mistakes in our lives. With some students, I used a quote that is often credited to Albert Einstein that says, "The definition of insanity is doing the same thing over and over again and expecting a different result." I would suggest that the student write down concrete steps they would follow so that they could accomplish their resolutions. It was important for them to list the different steps they planned to take to avoid getting the same unsatisfactory grade from the past. I'd remind them that each resolution will fail unless concrete steps are taken to make them happen. A resolution without action is likely to have the same outcome as not doing anything to make a dream come true.

Students really learned that resolutions need hard work so that they do not remain just hopes or wishes.

Resolutions are needed within relationships if they are to remain healthy. Everyone is different and these differences may be the cause of many conflicts. Disagreements in themselves are not bad; what is bad is the conflict that sometimes arises because of them. For instance, my husband and I have differing opinions about almost everything. If we allowed our opinions to divide us, that would likely be the end of our marriage. But no matter the difference, we work toward finding a resolution. Sometimes I give in, but sometimes he does too. We have remained together for as long as we have because we remember that a difference is not a reason to stop loving each other. We attempt to respect each other even with our different perspectives. Early on in our marriage, we made the decision to never go to bed angry at each other.

Similarly, when the girls were teens, we would regularly have different points of view. I tried to listen to their perspectives, sometimes coming up with a compromise. Other times, I put on the adult hat and would say that I was the parent and therefore I had the obligation to do what I thought was best for them and our family. For instance, they insisted on wanting cell phones as young as ten years old. I listened to their rationale for why they thought having a cell phone was essential. After listening to them, I found a resolution to our varying opinions of whether they should have a phone or not. I said, "I understand that others in your classes have phones. However, I have analyzed the issue and have concluded that the phone should be for necessity and safety, and not just because others have them. Therefore, I believe that a phone is not necessary for you until you go to high school where you might have to communicate with me for transportation issues or for safety when you walk to and from school some days." They attempted to change my mind, but when they heard my reasons and explanations of when they would get a phone, the issue was resolved.

Communication is important for any chance of conflict resolution. Both parties need to be open to hearing each other. Communication isn't just about speaking our own point of view, but it must also include listening to the other person's perspectives. At work, on the rare occasion when there was conflict between me and a coworker, I would try to understand their point of view. After listening to them, I would change my mind at times, but other times I would simply say, "I respectfully disagree with you." I wanted my coworker to know that even when I didn't agree with them, it didn't mean that I stopped liking them. We would both understand each other because of our communication, even if we remained with opposing opinions. The resolution is sometimes to respectfully disagree.

My mom used to always tell me that the only thing without a resolution was death. She believed that everything else had a solution. This may be why she insisted on doing anything medically possible that could be done to help me walk. She never gave up, and for that I am grateful. As an adult, at times I have sometimes questioned if there are ever situations that can never be resolved no matter what is done. For example, although I had numerous surgeries to "fix" my inability to walk, the damage polio did could not be resolved. Though I walked for a few years with braces and crutches, the weakness of my legs could not be resolved, so as a result I have been a regular wheelchair user. Still, I am glad that my mother lived to see me walk because she wished and prayed for it so much. It was more her wish than mine. I never aspired to walk, especially not by having to wear uncomfortable braces and crutches. I am just gratified knowing that my mom's dream became a reality and that, in her eyes, the persistence paid off by finding a resolution for my paralyzed legs.

Sometimes problems are so great that there really may be no resolution to them. I know I had my share of disappointments when I worked so hard to support a student, then felt that I failed to make the difference I wanted. It was never because of my lack of effort or hard work, but simply because it was not a problem for me to resolve. For instance, I had a student who came in with a condition that left him completely paralyzed except for his ability to move his eyes. He was on a ventilator and unable to talk or do anything independently without his nurse. He had had an aneurism when he was seventeen, which caused this condition.

The student had done well academically in high school, and he had been a stellar athlete, but now he was totally incapacitated due to his disability. When he came to Harper and met with me, he was hoping to attempt college, and I so wanted to make that possible for him. I worked tirelessly trying to figure out how he could be accommodated so he could enroll in classes. I was persistent in trying to make impossibilities possible by reading as much as I could about his diagnosis.

In my research I found out that his disability is a very rare condition, affecting only about twenty individuals in the entire nation. Without his ability to communicate, the options were nonexistent. Even when I sought support from my colleagues, no one in my department was able to find a reasonable way to accommodate him, even for taking his placement exams. He used a device with a color/number technique for communicating, but very few people knew how to use it and it was difficult and tedious to learn. I was even willing to try to learn his communication technique but found that it took over twenty minutes just to ask him one question. I was disappointed, but no matter how much I wanted to help him, we just didn't have the technology or personnel to help him.

My hope is that this student will find his way and that a solution can be discovered that will allow him to go to college. Technology advances rapidly, so I am betting on new technology that will facilitate his ability to communicate in the near future. Also, the human potential is limitless, so again, I just hope that this student finds a way to get a higher education despite his multiple limitations and disabilities. Perhaps there is a specialized school that can offer him the level of support he needs.

Sometimes if there is no solution, it probably is a problem that cannot be resolved. The only thing left to do is to accept the truth. In our lives, we will encounter many problems that we want to resolve. Many of them will be resolved with patience and determination; some will not be resolved no matter what we do. For example, back to my disability, though getting me to walk was never resolved, that didn't mean that I couldn't find a way to be mobile and successful in reaching my goals. In my wheelchair, I am quicker than many people, and though some may think of it as me being "confined" to my wheelchair, the truth is that I am free and independent in it. By no means am I confined. Again, though my problem was not resolved, I found acceptance and a way to make my mobility possible.

Some solutions are possible if we get creative. For as long as I remember, my mom had been a gardener. I always saw it as a hobby for able-bodied individuals, especially after observing the hard work that it required. However, when I no longer had my mother, and I wanted a garden, I found a solution. It just required some investment and the help of family and friends to make it possible. I now have a beautiful garden, and in my wheelchair, I plant, water, and maintain my full garden of vegetables and flowers. Solutions can be found. Though I may do my gardening differently, I was still able to find a solution that allows me to enjoy this hobby.

Resolutions require us to think outside the box. We cannot resolve things without being willing to try different methods of doing things. Just like I can garden, my husband who cannot bend his joints due to his arthritis is able to take care of all his personal needs independently. Sure, it might take him longer than it takes me to get dressed, but he does it. Similarly, it takes me longer to plant and water my garden, but I get it done. Even when the hose gets all tangled up on my wheelchair's wheels, I am patient and try not to get frustrated with the additional difficulties I go through.

We all have problems in different stages of our lives. We need to diligently work toward finding solutions. We must be open to possibilities, and to not get discouraged if we cannot find a solution, though I firmly believe that a solution can be found if it is in our destiny. It might not happen today or tomorrow, but it can happen. It is not a failure to accept that *we* cannot find a solution, because it doesn't mean that someone else can't. So, after all, it seems that I *do* agree with my mother's philosophy that there are solutions for everything except for death.

Sometimes someone we love says or does something that hurts us. We feel so hurt that we may believe that the relationship is destroyed. We may not see a resolution immediately. However, with communication, a better understanding of what happened can help salvage the relationship. If there are no possible resolutions because the hurt is too deep, then forgiveness may be the only solution. Forgiving someone doesn't mean that the wrong was not done or that it is forgotten. It simply means that the best resolution is forgiveness to let go of the pain so that peace can be found again.

To cultivate a plant, we must think of all the problems it has and make decisions about whether changes are needed. We need to resolve what we think is wrong. Perhaps the plant needs more sunlight, or it needs to be under the shade. The plant may need more water, or it may be watered too much. For example, my brother, Mon, gave me a money tree as a retirement gift. For the first couple of years, the money tree grew beautifully, but suddenly, leaves were beginning to brown, sap was oozing out, and it was evident that it was dying. I looked at it and thought of all the possible solutions for the problem. I determined that it had likely outgrown the pot it was in, based on all the information I gathered. I asked Mon to come to help me to transfer it into a bigger pot, since it was too difficult for me to transplant it on my own. Two months after it was transplanted, the wilting plant came back to life. Now my money tree is flourishing and growing beautifully again.

Our lives are more important than any money tree. So wouldn't it make sense that we do anything in our power to make it better? We might come up with a solution simply by reflecting on the issues. Just like I analyzed the problems with my money tree, we need to constantly reflect on our lives. This will allow us to determine what changes are needed to resolve any issue or problem that is in front of us. By doing so, we will feel better about our lives. By doing a detailed assessment of our problems, we can then develop solutions which we can implement as resolutions. Like the plant, we may come back to life, or we may help someone else to flourish. Life is a journey and should never be seen as hopeless. Above all, we are on this journey together, so it makes sense to make our lives the best possible and to help others to do the same!

REFLECTION QUESTIONS

1. What types of resolutions do you make and how do you ensure that you keep them?
2. What is conflict resolution like for you?
3. What types of problems have you had that you haven't found solutions for?
4. Do you agree with my mother's philosophy that everything has a solution except for death? Why or why not?

CHAPTER 19

SMILE

With the pandemic, what I have missed most has been seeing people's smiles because of the mandate to wear a face mask. Without seeing a smile, I lost a lot of nonverbal communication that, for me, is essential in forming connections with others. When the pandemic first started, I knew this was going to be an issue. As I was debating on what masks to purchase, I ordered a mask that was made of vinyl, thinking that this would help others to see my smile. Unfortunately, they were not comfortable, and the plastic kept fogging up, which defeated the purpose. I am relieved knowing that slowly we are getting back to normal. I will be happy to see more smiles!

Smiles are like windows to the soul. When we see a smile, immediately we build a connection that gives us the impression that we are safe. When we frown, it is the contrary, and we get the sense that we will not be accepted. A frown makes us question our safety. Sadly, in the busyness of our lives, sometimes we forget the power of a smile. Although it doesn't cost a dime, sometimes we don't share our smiles. We move quickly, looking down, or just being oblivious of those around us as we complete our errands.

Smiles are a sign of joy or at least an attempt to be joyful. When we take pictures, we always say "smile!" because we want to capture the moment as if everyone is happy. Most people give a huge smile, showing their pearly whites, when a picture is taken. I've noticed that when I smile, it not only makes others happy, but my own attitude changes to joy. Even when I am having a bad day, if someone smiles at me, my mood changes. Smiling is a simple way for us to connect with others. Unfortunately, there are not enough smiles going around.

Sometimes when I am sad, I make the decision to change my mood, while other times, I don't even attempt to feel better. But when I do want to change my mood, I look for sources that make me laugh or smile. Perhaps it is looking at special cards that have been given to me by family, friends, or students. Sometimes, I look at old family albums or movies. Immediately, I begin to smile. Even though whatever was making me sad hasn't been resolved, by smiling, the burden gets lighter.

I believe everyone has a beautiful smile. Regardless of any insecurities, the smile brightens our face, and it lets out a ray of happiness. Smiles, to me, are like the sunshine that plants need to grow. Before having to wear a mask, I practiced smiling anywhere I went. I would make eye contact, smile, and give a friendly greeting. It never fails that, when we do that, others smile back. The power of a smile is incredible.

Whenever I had an appointment with a student or family, the first thing that I did was to put whatever problem I had aside, go to the front desk, and smile. I am certain that this gesture made the students and families feel welcomed. Even the students who were resistant to registering for disabilities services often returned the smile. This helped with building rapport, and each student knew that they were important to me. Smiles are the first step toward a trusting relationship.

Some people rarely smile. I don't know what their reasons are, but I wonder if smiling would help them feel better about whatever is going on in their lives. Life can be difficult and sometimes it is impossible to smile. However, with effort, we can try to find a reason to smile. We all have something that we can smile about, even in our darkest moments, though it might seem impossible. My mother was someone who always found a reason to be grateful. Even when she was suffering, she was strong in front of us, smiling as if nothing was bothering her. Looking back, I wonder how many times she just pretended so that we would not be concerned. I am successful at smiling too if I stop feeling pity for myself. Even in our most difficult times, we can find a memory, something to be grateful for, or just think of something that makes us happy.

Smiles and laughter have the power to transform how we feel. It's silly, but sometimes I look for YouTube videos of children laughing. I also enjoy watching videos of people dancing. What is important is to not stay in the depressed state and to do something we enjoy that brings us joy. Because I am a people person, when I am feeling down with nothing to smile about, I call a friend and together we will talk about something we enjoyed in the past. The conversation takes me to a time of happiness, and at least for a while, I forget how I am feeling.

In my office, I had a collection of quotes, jokes, and images that helped the students to focus on something other than what they were struggling with at Harper. Because my office had magnetic walls, by simply using a small piece of magnet, I was able to hang up anything. I started with a small collection, but as time went on, I kept adding additional pieces. Students appreciated reading my walls, so much that they began bringing me pieces they wanted added to my collection. I told everyone that I'd retire once all my walls were covered. Indeed, by the time I retired, my walls had hangings from floor to ceiling. I know that this helped change the students' mood.

Sometimes, people do not smile because they are embarrassed, perhaps because of some characteristic that they don't find attractive. Sue, a student at Harper, had a facial deformity that was part of her disability. At first, I could tell that Sue was guarded and even self-conscious. However, as we developed rapport, she was more comfortable with me. Once I noticed that she smiled, and I complimented her. She blushed, but I know she was touched by the compliment. I told her, "Did you know that everyone has a beautiful smile? A smile is the window to the soul. You should open your window more often." I really meant it. She looked beautiful when she smiled. Sue immediately changed. She was more generous with her smiles from then on. All her concerns about her beauty disappeared and she was free to be herself in my office.

In my department, we served a large population of deaf students. Although I never learned how to sign, I found ways to communicate with the staff and students who were deaf. The smile was always something I looked for when communicating with one of them. I felt bad that I didn't know American Sign Language (ASL) and feared that they would get frustrated with me for not being able to communicate with them directly in their language. However, if the deaf individual smiled, my tension would disappear. I knew that they would be patient with me. We would exchange notes, or simply use gestures along with a smile.

Smiles, after all, are the best form of communication. It is a universal language that everyone understands. No matter where a person comes from, smiling means the same thing. It connects us to people. It allows us to show our appreciation for one another. It has the potential to break down any differences or barriers. It eliminates tensions between races, disabilities, or other differences. Everyone understands smiles. No further explanation is needed. Still, sometimes we hide our smiles instead of giving them away.

We need more smiles with everything that is going on around us. Life is difficult. People are struggling immensely because of rising prices of food and gas. Income is not going up, but the cost of living keeps getting more expensive. One way to help each other is to show our love for one another by just smiling. When someone smiles at me, I always return it. It opens the door for conversation. It unites us in a way that wouldn't be possible had we just remained sulking in our own worries.

Isidro does a better job at smiling than I do. I have noticed that wherever we go, he smiles at complete strangers. Using his big smile, he regularly will say, "Howdy." At first, I found it odd, and sometimes wondered if it was appropriate. However, when I see the reaction of people, it confirms my thoughts about the power of smiling. I've learned from him, so now I too try to look up and smile. So now instead of getting annoyed because someone is staring, I smile, and the person is jolted, recognizing that they were caught staring, and instead they return the smile. The annoyance I might have felt goes away.

I have always wanted to view the world as children do. They are so innocent and honest. They almost always have smiles on their faces. They feel joy most of the time. During one of the book fairs I attended when I was promoting my children's book *My Mom Rocks: Her Chair Rolls*, I saw a mom with two kids, aged around eight or nine. The mom noticed that the kids were staring at my wheelchair and quickly attempted to move them along to the next table. I noticed this, so I said, "Hello kids, do you want some candy?" The mom had no option but to stop at the table.

I started to tell the family about my children's book. I asked the boy and girl, "Have you ever ridden in a wheelchair?" They looked a bit startled and nodded their heads to indicate no. I noticed that they were still stiff, not frowning, but not smiling either. I then said, "Do you know how to ride bikes?" Immediately they smiled and said yes. I smiled too and continued my conversation with them, saying, "Riding a wheelchair feels the same way as riding a bike. Do you know how I know?" They just looked at me and waited for an explanation. "When my daughters were little, they would ride their bikes, but sometimes, I would also give them a ride on my wheelchair. They told me that it felt exactly the same as when they rode their bikes." Their smiles got bigger. The family bought the book and moved on. However, I kept noticing that the boy and girl kept looking back to my table. I was sure that they were processing what they had learned.

Using a smile, I have been able to have many teachable moments of disability awareness that would have otherwise been difficult to have without the other person becoming defensive. In that instance of the mom trying to pull her kids away because she was embarrassed by their staring, my smile helped me to teach the whole family a lesson. I know that parents are well-intentioned when they try to stop their kids from staring, fearing that it is impolite. However, I want parents to know that children stare out of wanting to learn and that they should allow the children to explore differences instead of teaching them to look away. I could have easily been angry and grouchy because of the mom's approach, but instead, using a smile, I taught the children and the mom that being in a wheelchair is not weird. Being in a wheelchair is like riding a bike.

The interactions we have with others can lead to conflict, or they can lead to an understanding. If we interact with one another with a smile, the result will likely be positive. If we don't, it will likely result in discord. So, my strategy is to always start with a smile. Even the tensest of situations will lighten up with a genuine smile. A smile breaks down divides. A smile should be part of all conversations, even situations where a conflict is being discussed. In fact, a smile can turn the conflict into a resolution. If there is conflict and both parties go into it as adversaries, conflict resolution will be unlikely. On the other hand, if both parties go in with a friendly smile, it opens the door to a resolution.

However, forced smiles that aren't authentic or genuine can make situations worse. I don't know how, but people can tell when a person is faking a smile. Looking at some photographs, I can tell when I was forcing a smile and when the smile was genuine. In forced smiles, I look different. My lips are shaped as if smiling, but no teeth are visible. In a genuine smile, my teeth show, depicting true happiness. I bet I can tell a fake from a real smile in others as well. Although genuine smiles are preferred, if all that is possible is a fake smile, then that is better than an expressionless face or a frown.

Smiling is up to us. We are all living difficult lives. No one is excluded from problems. Sometimes we may feel there is nothing to smile about, but a smile is always possible if we search for the opportunity. Smiling has the power to make our lives better. It is the best medicine for a bad mood. It is the best option when we want to get along. It is up to us. I will always prefer smiling over being depressed.

REFLECTION QUESTIONS

1. How do people's smiles affect your mood?
2. How do you feel about smiling at people you do not know?
3. What are some instances when you found it difficult to smile?
4. What can you do to help yourself and others to smile more?

CHAPTER 20

TIME

TIME CAN BE OUR FRIEND OR OUR FOE. WE LOVE TIME, BUT WE CAN ALSO hate it. A twenty-four-hour day can seem eternal, or it can seem as quick as a blink of an eye. Time can help us, but it can also destroy us. Everyone alive has time, but some have more than others. Some can live for a few years but accomplish more than those with more time in their lives. How we use time will lead to happiness or take us to misery. Since life is always complicated, we must make the most of our time right now because time might run out. Time is so powerful, especially when we least expect it.

Our perspective about time changes as we age. As children, we can't wait to be older. As adults, we wish we could stop time. We are humbled with age, and we see how much time is wasted focusing on things that do not matter. We discover that what fills our hearts is more valuable than what fills our homes. Unfortunately, we discover this often when our time is running out.

On one of my trips for a conference I had an interaction that really made me reflect on what I wanted and valued for the time I have in life. It was around my birthday, so when Stacey, a friend and coworker, and I went to a conference in California, she had a surprise for me. She scheduled a manicure for me. As I sat down to be pampered, a nice woman, probably in her forties, and I had a deep conversation about life. She commented on how expensive the cost of living was in California. She shared that some people lived in mansions while others had a difficult time even paying rent for an apartment. She then asked, "What good is having huge houses, expensive cars, fancy jewelry, and fancy clothes, if we cannot take it with us after we die?" I responded, "You have a point." She then painted a picture in my head that I have used regularly since then. She said, "When people die, there is never a U-Haul following the hearse. All there is is a line of cars with people who love them."

I have used the memory of this conversation on multiple occasions to help me prioritize what is important and what I should focus on with the time I have in this world. I do not have a huge house (though I do need more space for access), fancy vehicles, or anything designer. However, my life is full of family I adore and who love me back. I have made lifelong friends that I value more than any possession. After all, it's not what we have but who we have in our lives that really matter. I use my time to foster these mutually loving relationships because I want my hearse to be followed by many cars.

When my mother passed away, after her funeral mass there were miles and miles of cars as we drove to the cemetery. The memory of that interaction I'd had in California came to my mind, and it filled me with pride, because I knew that my mom had used her time wisely. People whose lives she touched all wanted to say farewell. I thought to myself, *I want to have that type of wealth when my time on earth is over.*

So often, we waste so much time doing things that, in the long run, end up being a waste of time. I try not to live with regret, but when I look back, I realize that, so often, my time could have been used more wisely. I forgive myself, only because I am aware that I didn't know better. I spent so much time wanting to be normal and accepted by people who didn't matter. I wasted so much time crying because I didn't fit in. Hours were spent wishing that I was different. I wish I could get that time back!

Of course, now I know better. Maturing allows us to value time differently. When we're young, we think that we will live forever, so wasting a day binge-watching Netflix is no big deal. When we get older, though, we learn to prioritize time better, knowing that each day is a gift of life. A birthday becomes a celebration of making it through one more year, whereas the young see it as a year closer to becoming an adult.

I know God is perfect, but I wish he would have given me this wisdom earlier. Oh, how much I could have accomplished had I not wasted the time I did. Now I cling to each day, trying to fill it with things that matter. It sometimes feels like a race with time. When we are older, we remember that no one knows the day or time of our death, so we want to maximize each day to the fullest. Each day is quicker than the previous. We look back and cannot believe how time flew. With the pandemic, for a while, I couldn't see many of my nieces' and nephews' families, and now that I see their children, I cannot believe they are toddlers. I tell myself that everyone aged except me. When I see pictures on Facebook, I am shocked that some of my nieces' kids now have mustaches. Time ticks nonstop, and when it stops ticking, it will mean that our time on earth is over.

What we do with our time is up to each of us. We can choose to do things that in the long run do not matter. We can also choose to do what does matter. We live packed days, sometimes filling each waking moment with work and other obligations, leaving little time to spend with family and friends. Of course, depending on the stage of our lives, sometimes the responsibilities of earning an income must take a top priority, but if we plan wisely, we can also use time to foster memories with people we love. Time can be balanced, but we need to reflect on what is important to us and not wait until there is no time left.

My mom used to say that there is a time for everything. There is a time for sorrow and a time for joy. There is a time for work and a time for play. There is a time to be alone and a time for family and friends. There is a time for illness and a time for health. However, sometimes we focus more on sorrow, taking the joy for granted. We choose isolation instead of spending time with our loved ones. We spend time with illnesses because we neglect spending time doing things that help our health. We are in control of our own time, and what we do with it matters.

It seems that each new generation is expected to have every minute booked with things to do. I notice how parents keep adding more activities to their children's lives. Children are in camps, sports, dance, music, and many other activities, leaving little time for them to be home. On the one hand, this is helpful for children who may otherwise be bored at home watching TV or playing video games. On the other hand, sometimes they are in so many activities that it adds stress to not only the child but also the parents who have to take them from place to place.

When I was a child, my parents did not involve me or my siblings in any after school activities. Of course, the times were different, and the resources were limited. I would just spend my time with neighborhood kids, playing whatever came to our minds while waiting for the ice cream truck. We had little supervision, other than my mom occasionally looking out the window to see where we were. Our time was limited to the amount of daylight. When the streetlights turned on, that would be our alarm to go inside. My siblings and I sometimes reminisce about the good ol' days and say, "We all turned out OK without participating in anything."

As parents, Isidro and I decided not to overwhelm the girls and ourselves by involving them in everything. Each year, Ariel and Ariana would choose one activity they wanted to try out. They were both in softball, but their interest did not last. They both tried gymnastics, but Ariana was too self-conscious to even participate, and Ariel decided not to continue. Both were in karate classes. Ariel continued, though only for an additional year, but Ariana did not. Music was tried, first with the violin and then with piano lessons. Ariana discovered her love of music and continued with lessons until the start of the pandemic.

But mostly, they preferred to stay home with my mom, playing on their own. They were creative, finding ways to entertain themselves. They often played school or what they called "store," where one would be the buyer and the other would be the cashier. Because my brother Rick, who lives across the street, has two kids around my daughters' age, they hung out and played together. They would grab clothing and homemade props, then dress up and videotape stories they created and acted out. Once, they even recorded bloopers of their performance. I laughed hysterically when I watched their creative videos. I am sure they will cherish these times because they were so well spent using their creativity to make lasting memories.

Packing their schedules with activities would have robbed them of the opportunity to spend time with each other, and it would not have allowed for as much creativity. Of course, sometimes I felt pressure from seeing how other parents had their children in so many activities, causing me to doubt if I was making a mistake by not involving them more. Because of the pressure I felt, I sometimes registered them for summer camps, only to hear complaints from them about not wanting to go. However, I rationalize any lingering doubt by thinking that if they had wanted to be involved in something, I would have gladly supported their interests.

As adults, we are just as guilty in filling our own schedules. Of course, retirement offers more flexibility, but somehow, as I look at my schedule, it's still packed with different events. Sometimes I am so enthralled that I forget to even eat. I know that I am my own boss of my time, but sometimes I feel I am a dictator boss. I am failing retirement miserably for sure. My only rule, which I have broken only a handful of times, is that I do not want to use an alarm. I am not a morning person, so I try not to book anything before 10 AM. But because I am not a morning person, I am able to stay up late. Sometimes I lose track of time, and when I look at the clock, it is already midnight. Gratefully, though, once I make the decision to go to sleep, I immediately doze off.

I am always amazed how time seems to stay still when we sleep. It's as if we cease to exist, at least for me. I hardly ever have dreams, and when I do, I forget them. I may have slept eight hours, but it feels like a minute. I am disappointed when morning comes because I hate the process of waking up. For this reason, I have never been a nap taker.

Thankfully, the day only has twenty-four hours. Otherwise, I'd put more pressure on myself to get even more things done. I always put unrealistic timelines on myself, as if I needed to get things done NOW! Although I have heard the stereotype about Latinos being late and preferring to do everything "mañana," that is not true for me. I am like a dog with a bone.

Once I have it in my mouth, I don't let it go. For instance, I wrote my almost three-hundred-page memoir in three weeks, and I am following the same pace for this book. Of course, no one is pushing me to work as diligently as I do. I put the pressure on myself.

Patience is not my virtue for sure. I hate when someone tells me "tomorrow or later." I feel like screaming because I do not understand what is so important that they cannot do it today. I realize that this is my issue, and I hope to someday improve on this. I feel like I must work, work, work. I have a difficult time allowing myself to just be idle. I know that I need rest and time to relax, but honestly, I get stressed when I am asked to relax. Even remembering my mom's words about there being a time for everything, I still do not want to waste a minute, and when there is something to do, I want it done NOW. I am certain that my approach drives some people crazy. Perhaps I do this to myself because I try to do only things that I am passionate about and that I find important. Though others may view it as work, because I enjoy it so much, I do not. Still, I need some cultivating in this area.

Though I am conscious of how I need to do better in cultivating the use of my time, I so often seem to fall short. My daughter gave Isidro tickets for us to go see the Cubs play on Father's Day. I told myself, "It will be a beautiful day so enjoy it!" I was trying to cheer for myself because I knew how difficult it would be for me to sit idle for a few hours. Although I understand baseball because I used to watch it with my dad when I was young, I still knew that I would be captive for as long as the game lasted. I did well with the first three innings, probably because I had bought snacks and we were all enjoying them. The remaining innings were more painful. I kept thinking I should have brought my laptop. The Cubs lost 6 to 0, so that made it seem even longer. I was so happy when it was over. I guess I will do anything for love!

Many of the students I worked with, especially those with attention deficit disorder, had the opposite problem than I did. They would fill their days with things they enjoyed, often forgetting to do the schoolwork they were supposed to do. Their time management worked against them. I often worked with them on strategies they could use to better manage their time. Many students had never used a schedule planner. I would offer different options for them to try. I also encouraged them to use the technology available on their smartphones to keep a schedule. At the beginning of the semester, I'd often help them plug in all the assignments listed on their syllabi to whichever calendar they were planning to use. We also talked about how they could work around their other obligations to find time to study. I suggested they use what they enjoy doing, such as hanging out, playing video games, and watching TV, as a reward after studying.

As part of their orientation to college, besides getting information that acclimated them to the campus, we provided them with calendars, stressing the importance of using one. Many students found the calendar useful and would use it regularly. Other students continued their bad study habits, which often resulted in poor grades. Time management is a skill that needs to be learned and practiced. I would be persistent in encouraging them to keep track of their time.

Time is a gift all of us have. Sometimes we take this gift for granted and act like we will live forever. We need to be honest and hold ourselves accountable. Setting priorities is the first step to really using time effectively. We can allow time to control us, or we can control time. Looking at our lives and noticing how we live will help us determine whether changes need to be made. What's most important of all, we must always remember that time moves fast and that we need to harness as much of it as we can to make our lives, and those of others, better.

REFLECTION QUESTIONS

1. What do you do to manage your time? Is it working?
2. Are there any changes you need to make to stop taking time for granted?
3. What is the biggest challenge you face with time?
4. Is time your friend, or is it your enemy, and why?

CHAPTER 21

UNIQUENESS

GOD'S INFINITE CREATIVITY IS DIFFICULT FOR ANY OF US TO COMPREHEND. He creates every single living being, including humans, to be unique. In a garden, every single flower is different. They may be the same type of flower and even the same color, but when we look closely, we will see their differences. Similarly, no two animals are ever alike. As humans, we are different in our appearance, our personalities, our beliefs, our hopes, our fears, and in the way we view life. Even identical twins may look the same physically, but everyone would agree that each twin is still uniquely different.

Uniqueness is a quality that should make us love ourselves, but most of the time, it is a source of unhappiness. We struggle with accepting ourselves as we are. We are constantly wanting to be like someone else, or worse, we want others to be like us. This often results in competition, driving us further apart. In earlier chapters, I have shared my views about how we often want to be what we are not, and how this is a source of unhappiness. This is not only true about our physical appearance, but also true in other aspects of our lives.

It must be true that opposites attract because Isidro and I are as different as night and day. When I say up, he says down. When I say round, he says square. Our preferences for food are totally different. Our views about health and money are different. Still, we remain together. We have been married since July 1, 1995, so it is obvious that opposites can get along and work together. I used to think that relationships had to involve two individuals that were mostly alike and saw life the same way. However, now I see that it would be difficult to live with someone who was like me.

In my life, I need the counterbalance to help me grow. Sometimes an opposing view will shine light on our errors and even in the way we think. What matters most in a relationship is mutual love. When there is love, there is respect and loyalty. When there is loyalty and respect, having a different perspective doesn't destroy love, but maybe it even strengthens it. Our great differences challenge us to be better. Having Isidro by my side has made me a better person in all respects. I work harder to fix my mistakes that often his perspective might highlight. If I didn't have him, I would remain in the dark, thinking that I was always right.

I think that the reason our marriage has worked is because we have accepted each other's uniqueness without forcing the other to change. I understand his views, and he understands mine. We respect our varying views even when we don't share them. He does his things, and he allows me to do mine. However, in what really matters, we support each other and often come up with an agreement that allows us to work together. When we raised our children, we often had to compromise, changing our viewpoints so that we could come to an agreement. Sometimes I had to be flexible, but sometimes he had to be the one to change his views. Respecting each other's uniqueness allows us to be united even when we are different.

Ariel and Ariana are also individually unique. I used to think that they were different because one was adopted and the other was biological, but my mom pointed out that each of my siblings and I are different, though we are all biologically from the same parents. Ariel is a strong, independent young woman who has her own strong views. Ariana is noble, hardworking, and has strong discipline. I love them both the same and see value in their uniqueness, even if at times I am challenged by their unique qualities. I am equally proud of both and am so blessed to be able to call them my daughters.

Unfortunately, our uniqueness is often not favored, accepted, or valued by ourselves and even by others. We always think that either we are better, and everyone should think like us, or that we are not good enough, wanting to be like whoever we envy. We hurt ourselves and others by not appreciating the uniqueness of people. It often results in hate instead of love, envy instead of celebrating differences, pride instead of humbleness, etc. This constant battle divides us further and further, yet we keep doing it over and over.

When I do presentations on disability awareness topics, I often start with a disclaimer. I acknowledge that I am not an expert on the lives of other individuals with disabilities. I am only an expert on my own life and my own lived experience. I explain that even with the same diagnosis, other polio survivors and I are still uniquely different. Another person with polio will not look or behave like I do. Other individuals disabled by polio will not feel the same about their disability nor will they be affected in the same way I am. Additionally, other individuals with disabilities who have the same diagnosis, no matter what it is, will be different. No two persons with disabilities are ever alike, although we often tend to clump them together as if the disability has caused them to be the same.

Of course, many of us who live with physical disabilities will have a shared lived experience in terms of lack of access, lack of acceptance, and lack of opportunities. But our views about life are different. Our views are influenced by the onset of our disability, our family structure and support, where we live, and the varying societal response to our disability. We are more than just the limitation people see, and that makes us unique. However, for some reason, stereotypes and judgments are constantly made about us as a group, instead of looking at us as unique individuals.

During the Q and A segment of my presentations, I often get questions that try to get me to be a spokesperson for the entire population of individuals with disabilities. I always remind the audience that I could give general responses but that the best approach is to always ask the individual directly.

In a recent training, a member of the audience asked, "I never know if I should offer help to a person in a wheelchair who I observe is struggling in going up a ramp or opening a door. What should I do?" Again, I remind the audience that the best approach is to ask the person directly instead of making assumptions. I go on to explain the contrasting views my husband and I have about our disabilities. As far as I'm concerned, I have been a wheelchair user my entire life since I contracted polio as an infant, so I personally always welcome the help from others when it is offered. However, someone who recently became disabled, perhaps because of an accident or a disease, like my husband, and who are now wheelchair users, may feel differently about the offer. With a later onset of a disability, the individual may be trying to be independent to deal with their new circumstances. For them, independence might be something they are fighting to keep in their lives. I conclude by stressing that the best approach is to always ask first. I remind people not to get offended if an offer is rejected, because it is likely not a rejection of them but rather a rejection of feeling dependent.

Similarly, I am one of millions of Latinos in this country, who are all uniquely different. Latinos come from different countries, and even when we come from the same country, depending on where we are born and the family in which we are born into, we are unique. Sure, we might share a similar culture, but we may express it in different ways because of our different experiences. Generalizing about one group does more damage than good. The key is to connect to each person to understand that one single person's experience. It never failed, that whenever I was the only Latina in the room, I'd be asked to speak about the Latino experience. That often made me uncomfortable, and I felt it was an unfair question. For some reason, people are asked questions to which there are no answers because we are just one person among a large group whose experience may be totally different than ours. I am only me so I can only represent myself. I can only speak for myself and my experience and no one else's.

Latino students and parents I worked with, for different reasons, appreciated working with me because I was a Latina. First, many times I spoke the language they spoke at home. Second, they appreciated the affinity we had because of being of the same race. They knew that, though we are each unique, I would understand their experience and most importantly their values. They never expected me to be entirely like them because that would never be possible, but they valued being supported by someone who wouldn't question their beliefs. They liked not having to explain themselves and sometimes even having to defend what they wanted. Generally, I would already know the culture, making it possible to quickly relate to each other.

I quickly discovered that being Latinx is not just about skin color. I had students who were dark like me but did not experience the culture because they were born in this country and their parents were second or third generation immigrants. Also, sometimes they were simply not raised as a Latinx individual. When I married Isidro, I lived one year in Texas, where he and his family lived. I found it interesting that, though they had the same skin color, their upbringing was different. Isidro's grandparents were from Mexico, but Isidro and his parents were all born in Texas. So, when Isidro's family would introduce me to others, they would often say, "Isidro married a Mexican." Of course, privately, I'd wondered, "What the heck are they?" They didn't even speak Spanish fluently. It wasn't until we moved to Illinois where Isidro interacted with my family that he fully learned Spanish.

Another common saying of my mom's is "Cada cabeza es un mundo" (each head is a world). This was to stress that we are all different and that though we may live together, we experience things differently, making us unique with our own perspective. This is so true. As I think about resilience, I sometimes question why our approach to difficulty is so varied from person to person. When something is going on, I seek support from my family immediately, eager for advice and help. Others isolate themselves and keep problems to themselves. Our approach to life and the difficulties that come with it is unique for each person.

Students with disabilities often struggled with their self-esteem. I would hear comments such as, "I'm stupid. I am ugly. I can't handle anything. Everyone else is smarter than me," etc. I sought to help them appreciate themselves, reminding them that the way they viewed themselves is not necessarily the way others viewed them. My goal was to always lead them to success, no matter what that looked like for the student. Success for them could be finishing a class and not dropping it. It could mean passing the class with a C or better. It could be making friends because the student didn't have any. It could be completing a certificate or degree. I thought that once they met with their definition of success, they would be kinder to themselves. I wanted them to appreciate their unique qualities, disability and all.

In the Humanistic Psychology class I taught, I came up with an activity to help the students see themselves as valuable. I got a bottle of water and taped a sticker to it that said "disability miracle cure." I taught this targeted class only for students with disabilities so that they would feel comfortable talking about their disabilities, knowing that everyone else in the class also had a disability so they wouldn't need to self-disclose. I started the class by saying, "You are all in luck! I brought the miracle cure for your disability." Their eyes opened wide with incredulity. I took out the bottle and continued, "Each of you will have the opportunity to take the bottle to get rid of whatever your disability is." I then explained that each person should grab the bottle and say whether they would take the miracle cure or not. But, if they opted to take the cure, it would also mean that every single experience they have ever had related to their disability would be completely eliminated from their past and memory. For example, if they met a friend in a special education class, they would no longer be friends. If they had participated in any activity related to their disability, it would have to be erased from their memory.

For the students who decided not to take the medicine, they had to explain why they would pass up the opportunity. The first time I did this activity, I hypothesized that everyone would take the miracle drug without a second thought. To my surprise, every time I did this activity, the class was closely divided in half according to what the students chose to do. After the activity, we would have a discussion to process the results. I would share that the disability was part of their identity and that it made each one of them unique. If they ceased to have the disability, their experiences, their viewpoints, their successes, and many other things would be different. After all, they were the person they were because of all of their experiences, including experiences they had because of their disabilities.

It was always surprising to hear students explaining why they would not take the miracle medication. Sometimes, they were so convincing that it motivated some of the other students to change their decision from a yes to a no. And even those who still would consider taking the drug sometimes shared during the processing of the activity that they would have to think about it, that now they weren't sure if they would take it or not.

It would have been irresponsible for me not to clarify that if a doctor recommended a treatment that could make their symptoms better, that they should do what the doctor recommended. But I also reminded them that there is no such thing as a miracle cure. The only true miracle available to them is learning to appreciate themselves with disability and all. Of course, I also participated in the activity. I always chose not to take the miracle drug, explaining that my unique experiences because of my disability allowed me to get to my current place in life and that I absolutely loved being with them, my students. No miracle cure was worth it if it meant that I would not have met each of them.

It is difficult for people who struggle to embrace their uniqueness, especially when what makes them unique is also the cause of their difficulties. No one wants to suffer, and any opportunity to stop the pain is readily welcomed. However, we do not realize that everyone suffers. And we suffer only because we do not accept ourselves as we are. We always want to blame something else for our struggles. At times, we feel that our disability is to blame, wishing that we didn't have it so that we could be like everyone else. Even those without disabilities always want something different. Sometimes they are overweight and want to be thin. Other times, people have curly hair and want straight hair, or they want to be tall instead of being short. Clearly, what makes us unhappy is seeking to be what we are not. Living without a disability, being overweight or thin, having a different hair texture, or our height is not the problem.

Sometimes, what we have, others want, though we might despise it. I'd often overhear my daughters' banter about their physical characteristics. My daughter Ariana has long, curly hair whereas my daughter Ariel has long, straight, silky hair. Ariana would complain about her curls, saying that they were difficult to manage and that she wished she had Ariel's hair. On the other hand, Ariel always wants curls, using a curling iron to attempt to have them when going out to social gatherings. I always reminded them that they were both beautiful and that they should celebrate their uniqueness. Of course, they were smart alecks and always retorted, "Then why do you color your hair?"

We can always strive to be better, no doubt. But being better doesn't mean that we must be like everyone else. We need to accept ourselves, because no one else can ever be like us, and that makes us all singular. Loving ourselves and our uniqueness will lead to happiness. Loving and accepting others' differences will lead to peace.

REFLECTION QUESTIONS

1. What makes you unique from everyone else?
2. How do you feel about your uniqueness? Why?
3. What unique qualities do you appreciate in the people you love?
4. Do you struggle accepting yourself? Why?

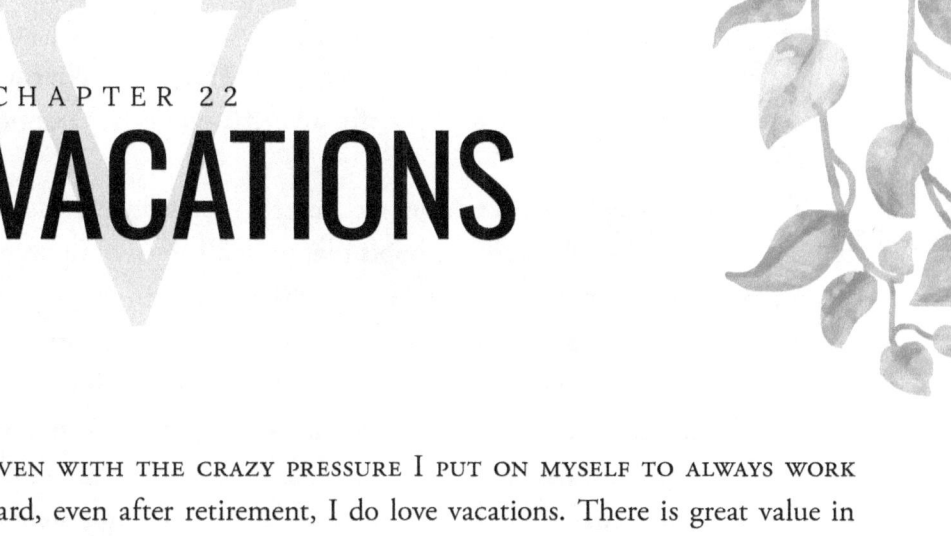

CHAPTER 22
VACATIONS

EVEN WITH THE CRAZY PRESSURE I PUT ON MYSELF TO ALWAYS WORK hard, even after retirement, I do love vacations. There is great value in taking time off from the routine of our lives to spend it with family making memories. Vacations do not necessarily mean traveling to exotic or faraway places. The United States is full of beautiful things to see and experience. Vacations do not have to cost thousands of dollars for them to be fun. Sometimes a staycation is just as enjoyable.

As a child, my family never vacationed. The closest thing to a vacation I ever got was going camping with my family. I enjoyed the camaraderie with the members of my family, but I did not like camping because I found the environment difficult while being in a wheelchair. It was too rustic for my liking, and everything seemed even more inaccessible. I couldn't understand why people enjoyed sleeping on the hard, uncomfortable ground. Still, I have very fond memories of our many trips to Beloit, Wisconsin, to spend a long holiday weekend as a family. My parents never went on these family trips, though. I wonder if my mom felt like it was a vacation for her when we all left for a few days.

While we were camping, I enjoyed watching my sisters cook. I was always amazed how they cooked all the same foods, including eggs for breakfast, over a campfire. They made all the traditional Mexican cook-out foods. The menu consisted of arracheras (skirt steak), primarily the meat of choice, along with all the trimmings and toppings to make tacos. This included pico de gallo, salsa, guacamole, Chihuahua cheese, and veggies. Of course, it would not be a complete meal without tortillas, grilled jalapenos, onions, and corn on the cob. I sure did enjoy the food. When it came time for dinner, we would all get a plateful and sit around the campfire, chatting as we ate.

The men would all go to a nearby creek to fish. I remember seeing my brother Mon wearing black rubber boots that went all the way up to his thighs. He would go into the shallow creek as the leader of all the younger fishermen. The creek was named Turtle Creek because of the many turtles found in it. After a few hours, the fishermen would return with a collection of fish they had caught. The thrill was in the catch, though, and not necessarily in using the fish as a source of food to eat. It was mainly a sport for them to see how many fish they could trap. Years later, though, some of my family members started cooking the fish on the grill and adding them to the menu for whoever wanted to eat them.

The kids, including me, would stay at the campground playing games, or we would go to a pool that the campground had for the campers. By that time, I already wore leg braces. I would sit on the ground to take them off, often noticing how other kids would stare. I would scoot to the pool, remembering how I always scooted on the ground of La Purisima, my pueblo in Mexico, before moving to Chicago. I would play with my little nieces and nephews. Richie, one of my nephews, even gives me credit for teaching him how to swim. Sometimes cousins and other people from La Purisima would join us. This camping ground became a hot spot for many people from La Purisima. Around the campfire, there was always someone playing a guitar while others sang along to the well-known tunes.

These are fond memories, even when I found camping less than comfortable. It helped us to have a change of scenery, and it allowed us to bond in different ways. The fresh air, the jokes, and the great company made our short vacations so memorable. We did not have extra money for vacations, so camping was an inexpensive alternative to take a break from the day-to-day life we lived.

Both Isidro and I value vacationing. Before having children, we went on a cruise and would regularly go to visit his family and friends in Austin, Texas. We drove, taking turns behind the wheel. The route became familiar since we went almost every year. While there, we would see his family and friends. Sometimes we would drive to San Antonio to spend a day at the River Walk, which was only about an hour away from Austin. Family would invite us to stay in their homes, but we always opted to stay in hotels so that access for both of us could be ensured. For our meals we dined out, and we always enjoyed eating at Isidro's parents' house. Isidro's father had worked in many restaurants, so he was an excellent cook. My favorite dish was milanesa (breaded chicken), and he also made exceptional tamales.

We both worked hard, so we always wanted to take the time as a couple to vacation. I was able to see all the different places he frequented when he was growing up. Sometimes, enjoying the good weather was all we needed to be happy. On several occasions, we rolled around on 6th Street, which is a strip of bars and nightclubs in downtown Austin. We loved to listen to the different bands playing as we strolled down this famous street. Isidro and I were not afraid to hit the road and venture to new places, both nearby and far. We learned about each other in environments that were fun, where we could be carefree.

After we adopted Ariel and after Ariana's birth, we spent the first few years staying put without venturing too far away. Still, we would visit family and entertain the girls by going to all the kid-friendly places Chicago has to offer. We took them to museums and parks and attended all the kid parties we were invited to attend. Sometimes we would simply enjoy watching the girls play in the yard with their toys and balloons, riding their bikes, or splashing around in a kiddie pool since we didn't think it would be safe to travel with them while they were still in diapers.

As soon as the girls were able to walk independently and understand our directives, we decided to start vacationing again. At first, I would ask a niece or nephew to come with us to help. We stayed close by, just going to places within the surrounding areas, still afraid of going too far while they were toddlers. We went to Geneva, Wisconsin; the Wisconsin Dells; and Door County before they were enrolled in school. Then we made it a point to go to Starved Rock and the other beautiful Illinois state parks. Our first vacation without another companion to help us was to Columbus, Ohio, because we wanted to take them to Kings Island, an attraction park especially fun for little children.

From then on, we always tried to take a family vacation at least once a year. We saved money throughout the year to be able to afford to travel, because we put great value on having family time in places we had never visited. We have gone to Florida, Texas, Las Vegas, California, Hilton Head, Tennessee, Missouri, most of our surrounding Midwestern states, Canada, and even Hawaii. We have also traveled to other countries like Honduras, Belize, Mexico, and Puerto Rico (when it was a port stop for cruises we were on). We even decided to purchase a couple of timeshares because we were pleased with the space and access resorts offered us. Besides, we knew that vacationing was always going to be part of our lives. We put high value on family time.

Vacationing is a way to unwind and spend time away from all life's stressors. My parents and Isidro's parents never vacationed when we were children, so Isidro and I decided that we wanted to give our girls a different experience. Vacationing has also been educational for the girls. Since we drive most of our vacations, they would enjoy the road trip, taking pictures of welcome signs whenever we crossed a state line. Additionally, they learned all about accessibility, often observing how we would struggle to find a hotel that could accommodate us. As a result, they became great advocates of disability access because of the struggle they observed us having when we traveled.

For work, I also had the opportunity to travel to different states to attend conferences. Although they weren't vacations, they served me the same purpose. It was a time to get away from work and learn about what other colleges were doing for their students. Most of the time I traveled with coworkers, so it was also an opportunity to develop close friendships with them. We would try to do something fun in the evenings, or we would just enjoy watching a good movie with chocolate and popcorn. I had so many laughs during those trips, giving me energy to return to work rejuvenated and with fresh ideas. I regularly presented at conferences to share the wonderful support Harper offered students with disabilities. Coworkers who traveled with me also learned about my access struggles, often commenting that traveling with me highlighted so many issues of accessibility and that it taught them to be more aware of the possible struggles of our students.

Several of my friends and family members have traveled to many locations out of the country, often sharing their experiences and pictures when they return. My immediate family and I have not traveled much outside the country, except for Canada, because we struggle with accessibility even in the United States where there is a law. We figure other countries would have too many barriers for us to navigate. I always asked my friends to evaluate the access wherever they traveled, and inevitably, they would share that access would be difficult for me.

I realize that not everyone can afford to take a vacation because of family obligations or tight finances. However, there are many things to do that don't cost much money. Most urban cities offer many festivals and free music concerts, especially during the summer. Visiting state parks is free, and they offer a lot of picturesque sites, hiking routes, and activities. Sometimes packing sandwiches and drinks for a picnic can be a meaningful experience for the entire family. How much is spent or where one goes is not what matters. What matters is taking a break and making memories that no one can ever take away.

Life can be difficult, as I have said many times. Sometimes we need a change of pace and scenery to appreciate one another and reflect on what is important. When my life on earth ends, I know that, with all the vacations we took as a family, I am leaving my daughters the best inheritance—great memories. I'd rather spend what I have on the family when I am alive than leave it for them when I die. I bet that both Ariel and Ariana would agree that this inheritance is more valuable than any material possession I could leave them after my death.

We deserve to have experiences that bring joy. Obligations, work, problems, and difficulties will all be here when we return. But perhaps upon our return, we will see the difficulties of our lives with a different perspective. Having a balance between work and relaxation is important for people to have the energy to continue with life's battles without feeling burnt out. Again, there is a time to work, but there is also a time to play.

Going on vacations is probably more challenging for individuals with disabilities like my husband and me, but the difficulties are blurred after all the fun times we have. For us, it is more difficult to adjust to new environments because we can no longer do the things in the manner that we can do them at home. For example, our resorts or hotels may have grab bars that are in a different place than where we need them to be. Also, the bed may be too high, or the towels may be placed where we cannot reach them. Still, even with these inconveniences and barriers, Isidro and I do not stop with our desire and need to vacation. Even after I fell and broke two bones on my vacation last summer, which I narrated in the Preface of this book, it has not deterred us from planning other vacations. Some view it as courage, but we view it as a necessity. Everyone needs and deserves a vacation.

Sometimes I am saddened when I remember that my mom never vacationed or did anything fun for herself. I even regret not encouraging her or facilitating opportunities for her to go to different places. To her, the idea of going away became a source of stress. I remember just a few times that she went away, but all of them involved visiting a sick relative. We were all thrilled when my sister Reyna, who retired to Florida, convinced my mom to go for a short visit. My mom resisted leaving her home, saying that she felt like she didn't belong anywhere else. She was set on her routine and found solace doing what she loved, caring for her family and gardening. If I could have her back for a while, though, I would love to show her how beautiful our world is. Yet again, from heaven, she probably can see it and is enjoying it already.

Traveling opens our eyes to different ways of living. Our world is so amazing and grandiose that no one in a lifetime can see it all. Sometimes I can get a glimpse of the beauty of our world from movies and the stories of family and friends. However, I am sure that what I've seen on TV and what has been described through the eyes of family and friends doesn't come close to personally seeing the different parts of the world with my own two eyes. I would be able to see how truly beautiful those places really are.

Just like I didn't vacation as a child, my daughters haven't experienced visiting other countries for vacations. My hope is that when they form their own families, they remember the great memories of vacations we had. Additionally, I hope that when they have their own families, they include traveling to different parts of the world. I want them to always remember to vacation and for their children to experience seeing our beautiful and diverse world. It is imperative to take time to vacation to see the magnificent world we live in. In doing so, our lives' quality will be much better.

REFLECTION QUESTIONS

1. What has been your experience with vacationing?
2. What parts of the world would you like to see that you haven't?
3. What are the benefits you have experienced when you vacation?

CHAPTER 23

WAFFLES

W<small>HAT CAN POSSIBLY BE THE SIGNIFICANCE OF WAFFLES IN OUR LIVES?</small> Well, it is the only word I can think of that starts with W that means the same thing in both English and Spanish! (Or at least the Spanglish word for it.) Even so, I *do* think that waffles add value to our lives. Freshly made waffles topped with melting butter, fresh fruit, maple syrup, and whipped cream are delicious. Now I want some. I bet I made everyone hungry!

In all seriousness, I choose waffles in this chapter to represent all types of food. Food doesn't just meet one of our daily basic needs; it also unites us as people. Whether eating dinner with the family, eating lunch with a friend, or simply enjoying food at a party, food brings people together. When there is food, people come. When there is food, there is bonding.

Food plays an important part in the life of a family. As a child in Mexico, we did not have the resources to have a variety of food, but we were never hungry. The traditional rice and beans with homemade tortillas were always on the table. My siblings fought to get the pan used for the refried beans. They wanted it to scrape the ring of beans that formed around the pan when the beans were refried. We enjoyed eating salt tacos. We loved the freshly made tortillas sprinkled with salt and rolled into a taco. We experienced immense joy when, on special occasions, a box of cookies was divided among us. Regardless of the extent of our poverty, we were always reminded that we were fortunate to have food to eat.

Immigrating to Chicago dramatically changed our access to food. My mom was able to buy enough food for each week, and she was able to cook a variety of dishes for the family. She regularly made her own tortillas and always had a big container of them for everyone to access for a quick snack. Her recipes were simple but delicious. I will never forget her fried eggs and her arroz con leche (rice pudding). My parents taught us to never take food for granted, reminding us never to waste food. Although we didn't have many meals all at once because of our different schedules, we were always together, and my mom always offered us food. She rarely took no as an answer. According to my mom, food was the cure for any ailment or emotional problem.

As I formed my own family, when the girls were little, we had dinner together. I would cook the food the girls liked, often making something different for Isidro and myself. I learned how to cook all my mom's recipes but added other recipes to my collection too. Others believe that I am a good cook. Our preference for food is uniquely different. I love spicy food, the hotter the better. Isidro loves vegetables, and his favorite meat is chicken. Ariel and Ariana like the traditional foods of teens such as pizza, burgers, and pasta. We are blessed that we have the resources to buy what we enjoy eating.

At work, I regularly brought in homemade food to share with my co-workers. During the summer, I'd bring homemade salsas that were made using the fresh vegetables from my garden. My bruschetta was also a hit. Our office celebrated birthdays, special events, and holidays with food. We always looked for an excuse to plan a potluck where we could all bring in food to share for lunch. We had cookie exchanges for the holidays. We always had food for student, faculty, or parents' events. Sometimes we would order lunch, just because.

Tom, the director of Access and Disability Services (ADS) for thirty years, started a tradition around food. He and his wife Barbara held a yearly chili fest, and he would invite everyone on campus who had supported our department and our mission by providing access to students with disabilities. Tom and Barbara would bring in several huge pots of different styles of chili, and everyone else in the department, including me, would bring an assortment of toppings. It was a celebration and a way for our department to show gratitude for partnerships committed to making the college experience of students with disabilities more equitable. Everyone enjoyed coming over for their bowl of chili while also mingling with people from different areas of the college.

We loved food so much that we started what we called the Breakfast Club. We would sign up to bring breakfast items for the whole office on Tuesdays. We brought in waffles, egg casseroles, and oatmeal, among other delicious treats. Although the Breakfast Club started out with just simple breakfast foods, it soon grew to encompass more elaborate meals. It seemed that each year our food selections became bigger and bigger, as if we were trying to outdo each other in a fun way. To better represent it, we later changed the name to the Birthday Club. We decided to sign up to bring food once a month to honor the people who celebrated their birthdays that month. I always chose May as my month, not only because it was my birthday month, but also to celebrate Cinco de Mayo. The menu was always Mexican food, which people looked forward to every year.

These gatherings with food connected us as people, regardless of the role we played in the department. Although we might have had different tastes, we always found something to partake in from the wide array of food choices. Some of my fondest memories come from the food we shared as a work family. Regardless of the stresses of the day or any conflicts we were involved in, during these gatherings we focused on each other while we enjoyed our food. This helped with the office morale, which always helps employees to feel more comfortable in the workplace. Having good workplace morale helped us to do our hard work and to be dedicated to our students.

Food adds flavor to our life in more ways than one. It has the potential to make us feel better. It is no wonder that, on bad days, we search for our comfort foods, whatever they may be. For some, chocolate is the best medicine for heartbreak. Some use food as medicine to treat feelings of depression or anxiety by eating an entire bag of chips, a pint of ice cream, or other types of foods good for binge eating. So long as it isn't habitual, doing whatever makes us feel better is preferable to staying sad and depressed. Of course, there are probably healthier ways to deal with our feelings than overeating. Sometimes the guilt of the extra calories consumed might backfire and make us feel even worse.

There is so much diversity in food. People are creative in figuring out different recipes to use with the available food resources of the area. For example, in Durango, Mexico, where I am from, there must be a surplus of poblano peppers. Durango and Chihuahua have a dish that is not commonly found in other Mexican states. This unique food item is called "chile pasado" (which translates to "past chili"). Chile pasado is poblano peppers that are grilled, peeled, and then set out to dry. After they dry completely, they turn hard and dark. They're then ready to be prepared with meat, potatoes, or just cheese. I am sure many might see it as gross or unsanitary, but it is loved by many people in those states, and I am one of them.

Sometimes the grossest sounding foods are delicacies in some places. In some states of Mexico, it is common to eat certain bugs. This is true for other countries as well. I suppose our ancestors figured out how to survive and used whatever was available, which later became a cultural dish. In many states of Mexico, one of the tastiest types of soups is called menudo, which is soup made from tripe. The tripe is carefully washed and cut into pieces to be boiled for hours so that it can be made into a soup. Another food that some may find unappealing is lengua, beef tongue, like I mentioned in an earlier chapter. However, for the people who consume these foods, there is nothing gross or strange about them.

For some people, food becomes an enemy. Some develop difficulties moderating the amount of food they eat. Some cannot control how much they eat, and some do not eat enough to receive the nutrients the body requires. This results in severe medical issues because of eating disorders. Over the years, I worked with several students with eating disorder diagnoses. I remember one student who, even though she was under treatment from a professional psychologist, was still constantly battling her eating disorder. If the student hadn't addressed the issue, it could have caused significant health complications and even death. My student weighed well under one hundred pounds, and she was tall. With professional help, she understood that her eating disorder was serious and was working hard to control it.

Another problem that has gotten out of hand is that more Americans than ever are overweight or obese. This is even more concerning for children. Commercials on TV lure children into craving foods that are not well balanced or healthy. To complicate things even more, low-income status families cannot afford healthier choices for their children. A quick McDonald's meal is affordable and available at any time compared to the double cost of buying fresh vegetables and fruits. Children are bombarded with commercials promoting fast food. Portions are bigger for little or no additional cost, so families are allured and see it as a bonus to get the largest portions.

Vegetables, organic options, and items for a well-balanced diet are too expensive for families that live paycheck to paycheck. Families are also working long hours to make ends meet, so they prefer to purchase food that can easily be prepared for their children. Even if these parents wanted to prepare healthy meals, they do not have the time because of work and they cannot afford the additional cost. The options are limited, so having unhealthy foods ends up being better than not having food at all.

Obesity is a real concern, not for aesthetic reasons, but because of the health consequences it causes. The likelihood of developing conditions such diabetes, heart issues, and high blood pressure go up the more obese a person is. Not only does eating too much and not eating healthy, balanced meals cause obesity, but an added problem is the lack of physical movement. With TV, video games, and computers, people spend more time in a sedentary position. Although many public fitness centers are available, the cost may be a barrier for some people to take advantage of them. Not to mention, personally, it is hard to find a facility that would provide the access I need. I have yet to find a gym that has a pool with a lift.

Because of my disability, I have had weight issues most of my life. First, I cannot exercise. Doctors have warned me not to exert myself, because I may cause damage to myself that would outweigh the benefits of high-impact exercise. If I overdo it physically, I may be unable to move the next day. Sometimes even going grocery shopping or mopping my home floors knocks me out for a couple of days. The only exercise I can do is swimming, and pools rarely have lifts for me to be able to use them. Second, I do not burn many calories because I am sitting about sixteen hours a day. Everything I eat can result in weight gain. So I do not eat a lot. Sometimes I only have a meal a day, which is also not recommended. I know I must change my eating habits because they contribute to the problem. And for me, the additional weight causes health concerns and also makes it more difficult for me to transfer in and out of the wheelchair.

Food is a blessing, but unfortunately, not everyone is blessed with it. Food insecurity happens in most communities. We do not have to go to Africa to find someone suffering from hunger. Sometimes it is right in our neighborhood. So, although food brings joy, the lack of food brings hunger and unhappiness. It is important not to take food for granted because the food we waste would be a miracle for some families. Food brings us together and gives us joy. However, not everyone experiences this unless we do what we can to help feed the hungry. Instead of buying a Starbucks coffee, we could donate that $5 to a food pantry. Imagine if everyone did this every week. It is our choice. Someday, we could be on the opposite side of the spectrum. We never know.

REFLECTION QUESTIONS

1. What recipes are most important in your family?
2. How does food play a role in your life?
3. How can you help those with food insecurity?

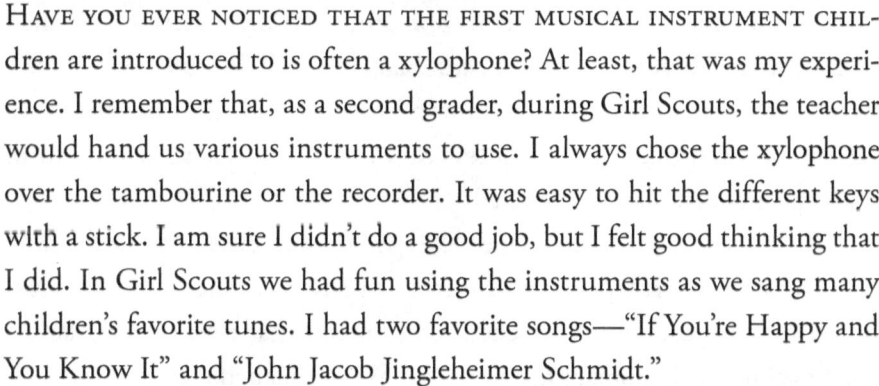

CHAPTER 24
XYLOPHONE

HAVE YOU EVER NOTICED THAT THE FIRST MUSICAL INSTRUMENT CHIL-
dren are introduced to is often a xylophone? At least, that was my experience. I remember that, as a second grader, during Girl Scouts, the teacher
would hand us various instruments to use. I always chose the xylophone
over the tambourine or the recorder. It was easy to hit the different keys
with a stick. I am sure I didn't do a good job, but I felt good thinking that
I did. In Girl Scouts we had fun using the instruments as we sang many
children's favorite tunes. I had two favorite songs—"If You're Happy and
You Know It" and "John Jacob Jingleheimer Schmidt."

Music is essential to life. It is a gift that touches everyone's heart. Even
when a person doesn't have a musical talent like me, music is appreciated.
The types of music are endless, so everyone can find music that they like.
It is interesting to see the history of music and the progression that comes
from the increasing sophistication of technology of each new generation.
Music can easily transport us to happiness, but it also has the power of
bringing tears to our eyes. People use music to dance, express feelings,
exercise, sing, worship, entertain, relax, and a multitude of other activities.

In high school, I was part of the band as a clarinet player. I intellectually learned how to read music notes. I also memorized the finger

placement for each note. However, because I am not musically gifted, it was like memorizing the dates for a history exam and not something that came naturally to me. I am not able to play a single note on my own and when I hear an instrument playing, I am not capable of distinguishing what notes are sounding. Even with my lack of talent, I still love music.

Disability and all, I love to dance, even if it is from my seat. I have always thought that if I had two good working legs, I would be a top-notch dancer. When my nieces were little, I taught them how to dance, explaining the steps they had to take. Intellectually, I know the steps for dancing to different types of Latin music. I believe I would be an excellent cumbia dancer. I also know the required steps for bachata, salsa, and many of the ballroom dancing styles. It helps that I enjoy watching *Dancing with the Stars* each season.

Once, while I was meeting with one of my students, Daisy, the topic of dancing came up. I said, "Daisy, I know a lot of dances in my head, but obviously I cannot perform them." She processed my assertion and then said, "Give me directions to dance cumbia, and I will do what you tell me." I put on some cumbia music, and step by step I told her where to move each of her feet. She practiced a few times and then was able to perform the steps quickly. She was amazed.

My heart was so touched when she gave me a farewell gift right before transferring from Harper to a university in Arizona. She wrote the most beautiful card; each word touched me so much that twenty years later I still have the card as one of my treasures. What touched me most was that she had remembered the mini dance lesson we shared. She bought me a Lee Ann Womack CD because of the song "I Hope You Dance." Tears flooded my eyes as I listened to the words. As the lyric says, "And when you get the choice to sit it out or dance, I hope you dance . . . I hope you dance," I will never stop dancing, even if it is from my wheelchair. Daisy and I connected in a profound way. I am so proud of her because she keeps dancing her own song. She is now a teacher in Arizona and used my memoir as part of a lesson for her class.

Good music has lyrics that people can relate to. I am always amazed by the talent of some composers because they can express in music the feelings many of us have. As a young adult, I felt that every song was written about me and my search for love. Somehow, it seemed that every song always dealt with disillusionment or heartbreak. However, while Isidro and I were engaged, we used music as a connection because he was in Austin and I was in Chicago. Then suddenly, it seemed to me that every song was about love and the beauty of it. Love songs can express what people feel but cannot say on their own. It is like a friend who quietly sits and listens to your heart and commiserates fully with what you are feeling.

Music is used as motivation when people exercise. Whether in Zumba, dance, or other types of exercise, music energizes people to move regardless of the activity. I have used swimming for my exercise whenever it is possible. Twice a year, my suburb offers adult swimming for its community members. I have signed up for the class multiple times. To accommodate me, they even moved the class to the local middle school because that pool had a lift. I would get ready in the dressing room, then go into the pool, and I loved that music was always playing. Sometimes, the music was playing, and when I was about to stop because I was tired, another high-beat song started playing, motivating me to swim a little longer and to do more laps. I caught myself swimming with hand strokes that followed the rhythm of the piece. It's as if that was the expectation. Every week, I owed music the credit for my swimming several additional laps each workout.

Everyone who has heard me try to sing would agree that I should never do it. But I will admit that when I am alone, I still sing along regardless of my bad voice. I can't help myself. Give me a good Bon Jovi song on a nice spring day when driving alone, and I will sing my heart out, talent or no talent. I believe that music is a good stress reliever. A song makes us forget and we get immersed in the beat and lyrics of the music. Some people are not good singers like me, but it doesn't stop them. I admire when people are not self-conscious or fearful of being judged, not stopping them from singing when they are moved to do so. I will only sing when alone. Trust me, that is the best option. However, singing is good for the soul.

I am so glad that Ariana did not inherit my lack of talent for music. She is talented and with weekly piano lessons, she was able to memorize each song without the need to look at the sheet music to play the tunes beautifully. She can also listen to a song and immediately figure out the chords and notes for the song. When my mom turned eighty, she learned to play "Las Mañanitas" (the Spanish Happy Birthday song) and surprised her in such a touching way. She learned it without even knowing the lyrics. Ariana also has composed songs, giving each a meaningful title. I started a YouTube channel to have a place to collect them. Though she could have made a career out of her talent, she chooses to play the piano just for fun.

Music can also be spiritual. It is used for worship in most faiths. Churches have choirs that help congregations leave their worries behind to focus on the message. In a way, singing in church is like praying twice. Sometimes, when I am feeling blue, I will play some religious songs to help me through whatever is going on. Worship songs have the power to cleanse us from worldly problems as we focus on the words of the song. Even in the Bible, there are always references about the importance of song and music. At church, because I can hide my voice among the sound of others, I usually sing along if I know the piece. I have favorite songs that always touch me spiritually. Two of my favorite songs are "How Great Thou Art" and "Amazing Grace." Ariana learned how to play these songs on the piano knowing how much I loved them. Sometimes, out of the blue, I'd ask her to play them for me. On more than one occasion, I got lost in my thoughts and would travel to a place of peace as I listened. Somehow, those songs fill me with hope.

A good party can never be without music. It may be a live band, music blaring through speakers, or a DJ. When planning a party, music is always on the list of things to have. Whether it is cultural music or current pop music, a party is not a party without music. I imagine each part of the world has its own party music. In Durango, rancheras are the music of choice. Icons such as Vicente Fernández, who recently passed away, will always be part of the repertoire. The occasion for the celebration or the common age of the invitees will likely influence the decision of what music to play. Music entertains young and old, males and females, regardless of the culture. Music is a universal way to celebrate life.

Music can help people relax. Listening to favorite playlists, soft songs, classical music, or wordless tunes often help take away any tension a person might feel. I had a student, Peter, with attention deficit disorder who swore he could not do schoolwork without music. I asked what type of music and was shocked to learn that he used hard rock. I asked Peter, "Isn't it too loud?" He smiled and said, "That's why I stay focused. The music doesn't allow me to think of anything other than what I am doing, and the music." It isn't surprising that music has been approved as a reasonable accommodation. At Harper, some students request to have headphones with music when taking a test. I remember discussing it with the team and coming up with a procedure to ensure test security. We approved it as an accommodation so long as the student showed that the music they were planning to use was legitimate and not a recording of the answers of the test.

Music speaks a universal language. One of the seasons of *Dancing with the Stars* included Marlee Matlin, an award-winning Deaf actress who also is an alumna from Harper College. She was able to participate using her senses. I was so impressed with her talent and ability to be a competitor with other hearing counterparts. This demonstrated that there is so much more to music than sound and the ability to hear it. It is much deeper than that. It has tremendous power to unite us in a way that nothing else can. Regardless of any differences, music allows us to bond as people.

Often, I think about how I use music for different emotions. When I lost my mother, I made a playlist to mourn her loss. Songs like "Wind Beneath my Wings" by Bette Midler, "Over the Rainbow" by Israel Kamakawiwo'ole, and "Supermarket Flowers" by Ed Sheeran made me cry more than once. I also had my playlist of Spanish songs that included some of my parents' favorite songs. This playlist had the same effect on me. Sometimes, we need to cry, and music helps us do that. I listened to the sad playlists for about a year because I missed my mother profusely. I still have the playlists on my phone, but I do not play them often anymore. I realized that, at the time, I needed the playlist to allow the tears I needed to shed to flow. Now, when I listen to them, I just feel a longing and miss her so much.

Music is timeless. Artists could have died but their music continues. I sometimes think about how fortunate these artists were. They leave their legacy behind with their music even when they cease to exist. There are so many unforgettable musicians that mark our world. Many artists who are no longer a part of our lives continue to entertain us long after their deaths. We enjoy musicians like Elvis Presley, Whitney Houston, Prince, George Michael, Michael Jackson, Selena, Juan Gabriel, Vicente Fernández, and the list goes on, because their music is timeless. Just like them, we should all strive to leave our mark on the world.

Music is a gift that has greatly influenced our lives. I cannot imagine a world without music. It adds so much color and flavor to our existence. We need to value music and appreciate each way that it helps us through our journey in life.

REFLECTION QUESTIONS

1. What kind of music do you like, and why?
2. How do you use music in your life?
3. When have you benefited from music?

CHAPTER 25

YOGA

I AM USING YOGA HERE TO REPRESENT THE IMPORTANCE OF ENGAGING IN wellness activities that help us live healthier lives. The only time I attempted to do yoga was when we had a person come to Harper to teach students with disabilities how to do adaptive yoga. I know several individuals with physical disabilities, sometimes with more limitations than I have, who do yoga. Some of my good friends without disabilities do yoga, and they always speak of how beneficial it is for them. I always listened and appreciated what they shared, but never saw it as a possibility for me. I know I probably have wrong opinions of what is expected, and I am fully aware of adaptations that can be made, but it just never motivated me to try it.

Each of us must find activities that help with our well-being. Yoga is just one option. Others prefer more rigorous physical activities, while others like meditation. We are all here for a certain time in life, though we don't know for how long, and it is up to us to strive to be as healthy as possible regardless of the duration. I admit, in full disclosure, that I have used my disability as an excuse. I tell myself things like, "I can't do yoga because I can't get up from the floor. I am not strong enough. I will look stupid. It doesn't feel safe for me because of the curvature of my spine. I can't do that. How could that help me? It's going to be a waste of time," and a multitude of other self-defeating thoughts to discourage me from participating in these types of wellness activities. I'm sure I am not the only one with these types of ideas that discourage us from doing what is best for our health.

Having a physical disability does limit us in the types of wellness activities we can do. It is not an excuse. It is true. On beautiful days, Ariana goes for walks. Even if I wanted to join her, how much exercise would I get from moving the joystick of my wheelchair? None. When we have gone on vacations, all the hiking paths do not matter to me because even in the best trails, they are not safe for people in wheelchairs, and again, no exercise would be obtained anyhow. I cannot participate in waterparks or go skiing. I am not able to go into the ocean and jump waves. I am not able to climb stairs to add more steps to my routine. Swimming seems to be the only exercise I can do, and I cannot do it in any pool; I need a lift to be able to get in.

When I retired, I had all the best intentions of making changes in my life that could improve my health. I thought that I would find a fitness center with a pool that had a lift and go several times a week to swim. My goal was to approach my well-being the way I approach so many other projects. I have accomplished a lot of goals by being organized and using lists to keep track of all that needs to be done. I imagined that I would be able to do the same with my physical fitness. However, I didn't count on a pandemic that shut us all down. Those plans went out the window. The pool would have to wait a bit longer. Of course, I didn't expect the pandemic to last over two years.

I have heard other people without disabilities mention all the reasons they cannot work out. Some may say that their schedule does not allow it; others complain about the cost because they cannot afford to pay the fitness center fees. Yet others may feel that it is a lost cause because they are too overweight. Whatever our reason is for not working out, we must do our best to figure something out. Our lives are too important.

Wellness, of course, does not have to involve physical fitness activities. I believe writing helps me. I can process and reflect on my life. I can pinpoint areas that I need to work on. I can also put on paper what I may not dare to say out loud. I have always used writing as an outlet for my frustration for the many times I have been hurt. For as long as I can remember, I have done some form of journaling. Through this process, I sometimes discover fears that need to be addressed. When I lost my son, I couldn't share what I was feeling with others. However, through poetry, I was able to let go of so much pain and anger.

Similarly, my mom's passing motivated me to write the story of my life to pay tribute to her. I didn't know that in the process of writing, I was also reliving moments that I had suppressed to keep moving forward. I also relived many happy moments that filled my life with joy. Writing was an outlet that helped me with my well-being. In writing this book, the same thing is happening. People will never imagine how I have been challenged as I reflect on areas that I need to work on. Some areas of my life are way better than others. My hope is that readers will discover the same thing. I might not have burned calories, but I certainly grew stronger because of reflecting on my life.

Aside from writing, another newfound hobby that helps with my wellness is gardening. I had my yard modified so that I can have access to plants. I never thought I could do gardening, but I am really enjoying it. To my surprise, I am developing quite the green thumb. It probably helps me physically too as I wrestle with the hose to water all my flower pots. Last I counted, I have over sixty flowerpots. I also have healthy vegetables like tomatoes, basil, peppers, kale, and broccoli, that I have certainly enjoyed.

When I worked at Harper, it was wonderful to see that many students participated in activities for their wellness. I had students who were athletes and it served as motivation because they had to maintain a good grade point average to be allowed to play. For instance, Luke was a wrestler. He loved that sport. I enjoyed his enthusiasm each time he shared with me the way he felt when he wrestled. Although he had disabilities, on the floor mat, he was like everyone else or even better. He discovered wrestling in high school, and it turned his life around. He was no longer a kid to be bullied. He was admired for his great skill as a wrestler.

How thrilling for me to have helped a student that made it onto a professional football team! Keith had severe dyslexia and struggled with reading. However, he was a stellar quarterback. He joined the Harper team, when they still had football as a sport, and he did exceptionally well. Although he had many difficulties with his academic goals, he worked hard because he wanted football to be his career. He knew he had to maintain a good grade point average to keep playing, so that was his biggest motivation.

Keith was drafted to a university where he did very well. On Valentine's Day one year, I received a call from Keith. He said, "Remember me?" In a thrilled voice I said, "Of course. How can I forget you?" I could sense his joy. He continued, "Guess what?" I didn't respond and just waited for him to tell me his news. "I just signed a contract with the San Francisco 49ers. I must go out of the country first for practice, and depending how I do, I might be on the roster in a year or two. You and my mom are the first two people to know this. I just had to call you because I wouldn't have made it without your help." I couldn't believe it. I congratulated him and reminded him that I knew he could do great things. Keith found his passion and a way to remain in good health.

Isidro is a big believer in exercise. I admire how, even with his lack of range of motion in his joints, he figures out how to work out at home. He stretches and lifts five-pound weights with his arms. Although he can't do sit-ups, I observe how he modifies them and finds a way to adjust them for his needs. He works out while listening to any podcast that interests him. He does motivate me to want to do something; however, our disabilities are complete opposites. I am flexible and can bend with little effort. However, because of the effects of polio and a diagnosis of post-polio syndrome, if I want to maintain the little strength I have, I cannot do strenuous exercises. I tease Isidro and say, "You work on your body. I'll work on my brain."

Not every sport or activity will fit our interests. What is important is to find something that does and to actively do it for our well-being. One of my sisters has developed a new interest in painting. Tere never painted before, but now she uses acrylic paint and paints landscapes of beautiful scenery. She tries to develop new techniques by watching videos online. She has told me that it relaxes her and keeps her mind occupied. Another sister, Kika, has also been painting by using a fan to blow the paint on canvas. She gives the paintings as gifts. She is even considering developing a website, with my help, where she could sell some of her paintings.

It is not always the case that we find productive ways to improve our health or well-being. Sometimes we make unhealthy choices when we search for what makes us happy. We might resort to overeating, smoking, taking drugs, or other unhealthy diversions. Some believe that eating a bag of chips or eating a pint of ice cream will reduce anxiety or tensions. As a result, the person may develop significant weight issues or, worse, other life-threatening conditions. Sadly, the problem for which a person binge eats does not go away.

Smoking is another habit that people assert makes them feel better. This is another unhealthy choice for the quest of well-being. The tension might be reduced for the minutes the person spends smoking, but it is a temporary fix. Just like smoking, doing drugs results in the same outcome. The fix temporarily helps with feeling better. However, once the effects are over, the person will realize that things did not improve. At this point, people look for the good feeling of being high more frequently. At the end, the difficulty is still there, but an additional problem has now developed, an addiction.

I met many students who admitted using drugs to make themselves feel better. Ryan had just gone through rehab when we started working together. He was very open about sharing why he started using drugs. His multiple disabilities, which made school difficult for him, and his parents' pending divorce was too much for him to handle on his own. He shared that he started using marijuana recreationally, but soon began to depend on it. It got to the point where he needed a joint constantly. It made it difficult for him to focus on anything else. He missed school a lot and his grades got worse. His parents, though now divorced, gave Ryan the ultimatum of going through rehab or leaving the house. The parents were sure that, depending on Ryan's decision, they were ready to follow through with the ultimatum. He decided to go to rehab, though he knows that drugs will be a constant temptation. The parents' tough love approach helped him see that he needed professional intervention for his addiction.

Gambling is also an unhealthy way to address difficulties in life. Some men and women look for the thrilling feeling that comes with gambling. Each time they decide to gamble, they believe that they will hit the jackpot. However, they also know that the casinos are set to win. Unfortunately, this does not deter them from their quest for a thrill because they crave it over the stress, tension, problems, and difficulties they experience in their daily lives. While trying to fix their difficulties, they develop an addiction that is even worse. I have heard horror stories of people losing their homes and all their savings because of a gambling addiction.

Another addiction, though newer, is addiction to video games. Many college-aged individuals spend hours upon hours in front of a screen, losing track of time and their other responsibilities. They love getting lost and forgetting everything that makes them unhappy. Yet again, the problems remain, but there are additional issues to contend with in their lives. It was common to have parents in my office who complained about their student's addiction to video games. They would say that their children stayed up until dawn while playing, leaving them tired and with little energy to do anything else, especially work or school.

When they shared these concerns, I would address the parent's approach for dealing with their child's addiction. One time, a loving mom and her son Tim came to my office. Tim had been at a university but was dismissed because of his poor academic record. Mom said, "Tim spends hours upon hours playing his video games. I don't know what to do. He doesn't work and barely attends classes, failing them all and making little academic progress." I listened carefully to everything the mom shared, all the while, the son was immersed in his handheld electronic video game. In front of Tim, I asked the mother, "Who pays for his video games, the internet, and his hand-held toys?" I already knew the answer but waited for the parent to respond. "We pay for everything because he doesn't work," she responded. Taking a risk, I concluded, "Well, that might be the problem.

If I could sit all day having fun and not have to worry about paying for anything, why would I want to work or get an education?" I am sure this was not pleasant for the mom to hear.

Sometimes, as parents, we need to support our children in finding healthy alternatives for handling the multitude of problems they feel they have. And, as parents, it is our responsibility to guide our children to more worthwhile, healthy activities. If we provide funds for them to partake in addictive vices, it is equally our fault. I recognize that parents are put in a very uncomfortable position. We never want to push our children out. We want their well-being, their happiness, and of course, their success in school and life. When we show discipline, our children might not like it and they may even be mad, but in the long run, it is for their own good. I always reminded parents to avoid threats that they could not follow through with when disciplining their child. For example, Tim's family were not willing to tell Tim to find another place to live, so I suggested not to use that as leverage. Rather, as parents we should always determine an appropriate consequence for a child's lack of meeting their responsibilities. For Tim, his mom decided that if he did not abide by time limitations on his technology, go to classes, and actively search for a job, she would cancel the internet and repossess all his electronic devices. She needed to be reminded that this rule might motivate Tim in better balancing his obligations, including getting his schoolwork done. I suggested that taking away his video games and stopping to pay for memberships that allowed him to play might be a good alternative. I am sure Tim listened to the entire conversation, but he never lifted his head from the video game.

Problems and difficulties will always exist in everyone's lives. We can choose to address them in healthy ways or make our situation worse by forming an addiction. There are endless options for everyone. The key is finding the perfect source of helping us with our well-being. Just like I use writing, others may use yoga. It really depends on everyone. Our lives can become unmanageable if we do not find something that could help us with our physical and mental health.

REFLECTION QUESTIONS

1. What activities are you doing to help with your well-being?
2. Are any of the activities unhealthy? How? How can you stop them?
3. What are you willing to do to maintain good health?

CHAPTER 26

ZOO

WE ARE FORTUNATE TO BE ABLE TO SHARE OUR WORLD AND TO COHABI-
tate with animals. Animals have been faithful companions to humans for
generations. Many animal lovers are activists and dedicate their time to advocating for the protection of animals, mostly on a volunteer basis. Others
choose to keep their own zoo at home, and the animals become part of the
family. Even those who are not animal lovers can enjoy a leisurely walk at
the zoo, learning about the amazing creatures that add beauty to our lives.

It wasn't until I had children of my own that I learned to appreciate
animals. As a child, I didn't grow up with pets, except for the chickens in
our corral. I don't ever remember going to a zoo until I was an adolescent
living in Chicago. My first six years of life, animals roamed the streets
of my little pueblo alongside me as I scooted around. On the same roads
where I scooted, there were men riding their horses and roaming pigs that
had escaped the confines of their owners. Men would regularly transport
their livestock through the dirt pathways of La Purisima. I also saw other
animals when my sister took me around town on her back.

When we came to the United States, we never had the opportunity
to have a pet. Feeding eleven mouths with a basic salary didn't leave
much room for the extra expenses of a pet. I remember my parents being

surprised with the manner others treated dogs just like if they were children. None of us had ever seen this behavior in Mexico. It was strange for us to see pets dressed in little clothing, though adorable. Sometimes my mom would say that Americans love animals more than children. She would base this on her observation that American families were small, with only one or two children, but it seemed that a pet was always included in the makeup of the family.

Because of my lack of exposure to them, I, too, struggled in understanding why anyone would want a pet. I thought that it just added additional expenses to a family's budget. I also questioned why owners were willing to pay astronomical fees for vet visits. Of course, I came to understand when I had my own pets and began doing the same things. One morning when the girls were in grade school, on the way to the bus stop, they found a scared little kitten hiding under a car. They couldn't resist, so they grabbed it and ran back home to bring me the kitten. They made me promise that it would still be there when they got back from school.

In the afternoon, when they returned from school, they found the kitten in a small box that I had put it in. I told them that they could keep the kitten overnight, but that the kitten had to go the next day. Well, the little kitten changed my mind. I didn't have the heart to let go of such a cute kitten. The girls named her Daisy. We took Daisy to the vet to ensure she didn't have any diseases, and fortunately she had a clean bill of health. Daisy was added as a member of the Herrera family, and Isidro and I loved the kitten as much as Ariel and Ariana. I won't deny that I even dressed the kitten with Barbie doll clothes, forgetting how strange that had appeared to me in the past. We even included her in family pictures. We had her for three years until a devastating incident ended her life.

One evening, Isidro went out to water the plants, not noticing that Daisy had gone out behind him. Daisy climbed the fence and went into the neighbor's yard. Our neighbor had a pitbull and, not knowing that our cat had escaped, she let her dog out. Our poor little kitten was mauled and seriously injured by the pitbull. The worst part was that, when we heard the loud commotion when Daisy was being attacked, we all ran out and witnessed her painful ambush. We were helpless and couldn't do anything without getting ourselves bitten. We just watched without being able to do anything. The girls cried hysterically. When the owner was finally able to pull the dog away from the cat, she locked him inside and went to grab Daisy from the floor, giving her to us over the fence. She was all bloody and barely breathing. We quickly went to our van to drive her to the nearby animal hospital. We were about halfway there when she took her last breath. It was too late, and Daisy died in my arms.

Although the neighbor felt awful and even offered to get us another cat, we were all still in shock and distraught. I was surprised to notice that I was sad not having Daisy anymore. I couldn't figure out when I had learned to love her. The house seemed different, and we were all mourning the loss of our baby girl. Ariel and Ariana didn't want to get another cat, saying that no one would be like Daisy. I didn't insist because I understood how they felt. I believe they were also scared of this traumatic event repeating itself.

A couple of years later, they indicated on their Christmas wish list that they wanted another kitten. Isidro and I were glad that the girls had recovered from losing Daisy, so we were happy to make their wish come true, especially because our neighbor had moved away with her pitbull. They looked online, and we went to a pet adoption event at a nearby animal hospital. Ariana and Ariel had picked a cute little brown tabby cat. At the event, we looked around at all the available pets, and as soon as I saw this one little long-haired white kitten, I fell in love with him. So, instead of going to pick up the one kitten the girls had chosen, we left with two adorable kittens, which we gave the names Rosie and Charlie. They are still part of the family; they came to us as tiny kittens and they are eight years old.

Again, I am not sure where my interest in pets came from, because suddenly, I wanted to get not just one cat but two. So, I began saying that I was a cat lover, but that I really didn't like dogs. I always commented on how difficult dogs were, convinced that it would be hard for us to take care of a puppy if we ever got one. The girls were happy to have the kittens, so they never insisted on getting a dog. Prior to the cats, the girls did have a few pets, though. They had fish, which somehow managed to die regularly. Ariana thought it was part of the process to flush them down the toilet. One day when none of the fish had floated to the top of their bowl, Ariana said, "Mom, can I flush it this time?" I laughed and said, "Ariana, the fish are fine. They did not die, so we do not need to flush them." They also had a hamster and even turtles. They had been responsible enough for me to believe that they could finally handle having cats.

My opinions about dogs soon changed as well. Ariel moved out, and when she did, she got a mini-Australian Shepherd dog she named Luna. A few months later, she decided to move back home, dog and all. Well, that dog has us all wrapped around her little finger. We absolutely adore Luna. I never thought in my life that I'd kiss animals, but love makes everything possible. I was saddened when Ariel got married and took Luna with her. I even debated whether we should get a dog of our own. However, I haven't because I want a dog exactly like Luna. I finally admitted that I fell in love with beautiful Luna.

Animals provide unconditional love to their owners. No one ever welcomed me like Luna. She would come and sit on my lap and watch me type. She would lick my face, including my ears if I would let her. She has the most beautiful eyes, one blue and one brown. I tease her and say she is half American because of the blue eye and half Mexican because of the brown one. I never imagined that I would feel the way I do over a dog.

On bad days when I am not feeling well, I get out of my wheelchair and try to rest. That is the signal for my cats to come by me and insist on being caressed and scratched. I cannot think of losing them. We got a little taste about how much we would miss them when Charlie escaped and was lost for several days. Occasionally, I like to look online and see what pets are up for adoption. I miss Luna and have a desire to have another dog, which is so surprising to me.

I have two best friends who are truly animal lovers, and now I understand why. My friend Bill is the king of animals! For years I would tease him, saying he loved animals more than humans. One day I asked, "Bill,

I notice that you are always drawn to animals you see on the street, but you do not do the same thing with children. Am I right?" In our banter he responded, "Animals are easier to love. Imagine what a parent would think if I wanted to pat and play with their children." Now, he teases me by saying that I have converted to being a pet lover.

My second animal lover friend is Veronica. She had such a zoo in her home, composed of multiple cats, dogs, and even a bearded dragon lizard. Those animals clearly brought my friend and her daughter a lot of joy. Unfortunately, this has been a tough year for my friend; sadly, four of her beloved animals passed away. The pets had lived a long life full of love but were aging and having health concerns. It was just difficult for Veronica to say goodbye to so many furry family members in the span of several months. She has created a mini-cemetery for her beloved animals where she pays tribute to them for all the joy they brought her.

The more that I am exposed to dogs, the more that they amaze me. They are so smart, forgiving, and loving. They ask for little in return and they never hold any grudges. Dogs are truly man's (and woman's) best friends. Even if they are scolded or punished, they still unconditionally love their owner. I have never seen such loyalty as I have from dogs. And pets bring so much joy. It is no wonder that dogs are often utilized by the helping professions. Dogs are used by first responders to assist with rescue. Additionally, dogs are trained to help with trapping criminals by sniffing for drugs. And they also are of great assistance in searching for lost children.

The disability community, especially visually impaired individuals and others with certain psychological disabilities, depend on animals to help with their mobility and their psychological challenges. Guide dogs protect their blind owners from danger, directing a clear path and stopping when there is foreseeable danger. Furthermore, dogs help people with certain medical diagnoses by working as service dogs or comfort/therapy animals. The ADA includes provisions for accommodations for students who may need the service of an animal. Universities with residence halls also have mandates that allow animals for use for therapy or comfort as directed by a doctor, regardless of any regulation against pets in the university's housing or dorms.

One of my students, Amanda, had a comfort cat for her anxiety. She wanted an accommodation to be able to bring her cat, caged, to classes. She said that the cat allowed her to relax when she was about to have a panic attack. Because the cat did not provide any direct service, the accommodation request was denied. However, if we had had dorms, and she wanted to have her comfort cat, she would have been allowed to keep the cat in her room regardless of any other rule.

Animals give more than what they receive. All that they expect is a home where they are fed and where they are safe. They are forgiving regardless of how they are treated. Sadly, some animals live in inhumane conditions where they are caged, hit, and sometimes starved. Animal breeders are after money and are not interested in the best treatment of the dogs they breed. For this reason, we should adopt animals in shelters rather than pay money to breeders to satisfy their greed.

Even nondomestic animals serve a purpose in our world. My dad was a firm believer that every living creature has a purpose, even the insects that sometimes scare and annoy us. We might not understand what their importance is, but from the tiniest ant to the most humongous elephant, they are serving a purpose in the world. Just like vegetables, plants, and the beautiful flowers around us serve a purpose. Animals should be respected, and everyone should be aware of the importance of animals in our life.

Sometimes we need a companion who will not judge but will love us unconditionally. A cuddle from a pet can help us during bad days. People who are isolated and live alone can find companionship with a pet. We need whatever tool it takes to live a peaceful and happy life. Sometimes an animal can help us reach peace and happiness. We need to respect all creatures, small or large, and acknowledge that this world belongs as much to them as it does to us. It took me a while to learn the benefits of having a furry member in the family, but now I am convinced that I will always need one in my life.

REFLECTION QUESTIONS

1. What role have animals/pets played in your life?
2. If you have had pets, how have they improved your quality of life?
3. Are you an animal lover? Why or why not?
4. What can we do to address the inhumane treatment of animals?

CONCLUSION

LIVING IS THE HARDEST THING WE'LL EVER DO, BUT IT IS ALSO THE GREAT-est miracle. The complexity of life makes it difficult to reach or maintain happiness. My hope is that some of the topics I have covered will lead readers to reflect on and analyze their lives. I know my life needs constant cultivation. There are definite areas that I need to work on, and some I excel in. The same will be true for each reader. Regardless of the benefits, I hope this book leads readers to healthy discussions about all that impacts us. We all share the experience of living. The more we can discuss issues of life to be unified instead of being divided, the better all our lives will be. I don't know how people will react to the many lessons I've learned. I just know that taking the time to reflect on my own life has helped me tremendously. I am better now than before I started to write this book. What I offer are not solutions to life problems; even professionally licensed counselors cannot do that. I just want readers to harness the power they have to take control of their own lives. The earlier we can do that, the better our lives will be.

Just like gardeners address the issues affecting plants, we also can do the same for ourselves. There is hope. We can live a better life regardless of the cards we were handed. We may not be able to change what causes us suffering, but we can change ourselves in order to become stronger and better able to handle our problems. We all have control over our lives. No one can ever take that away. What we do in the short time we are on earth depends solely on us. No one else!

FINAL REFLECTION QUESTIONS:

1. What areas of your life do you think you excel in?
2. What areas of your life do you need to work on?
3. What are some concrete steps you will take to improve your life?
4. Were you surprised with what you discovered through your reflections? Why or why not?

PASCUALA'S PERSONAL CREED

As a result of my reflection, I was able to identify the changes I need to make to have a better life. With my reflections, I developed my own personal creed, which I am sharing below. I make the commitment to visit my creed regularly and hold myself accountable.

I encourage readers to do the same by reviewing the reflection questions at the end of each chapter. The reflection questions throughout the book should guide you in the development of your personal creed.

In this creed I do declare . . .
I will accept myself entirely.
I will play more and work less.
I will smile more and frown less.
I will laugh more and cry less.
I will dance instead of sitting out.
I will not let other people's ignorance anger me.
I will make people whom I love my top priority.
I will make memories more important than possessions.
I will not only talk to God, but I will listen.
I will speak the truth even when it isn't heard.
I will be honest even when it hurts.
I will ask for help, but I will give it too.
I will forgive others, especially myself
And above all, I will live today as if it were my last day!